METROPOLITAN MYTHS

METROPOLITAN MYTHS

by

GLENYS ROBERTS

LONDON
VICTOR GOLLANCZ LTD
1982

Versions of the articles which make up this book appeared
in the London *New Standard*.

British Library Cataloguing in Publication Data
Roberts Glenys
    Metropolitan Myths.
    1. London (England)—Anecdotes, facetiae,
    satire, etc.
    I. Title
    920'.421   DA676.8.A1

    ISBN 0-575-03232-4
    ISBN 0-575-03154-9-Pbk

Phototypeset by Tradespools Ltd, Frome, Somerset
Printed and bound in Great Britain by
R. J. Acford Ltd, Chichester, Sussex

For P.K.W.H.

Contents

Preface

Metropolitan Myths first appeared as a series of articles in the *Standard*, London's evening newspaper. Like many things in Fleet Street, it was conceived over a good lunch with a perceptive Features Executive. The sun was shining, it was high summer and we were enjoying a glass of wine by the Thames.

So probably Keith Turner was only being polite when he asked me where I lived. He expected the answer to be Chelsea, which I abandoned twenty years ago as an alternative to suicide in my lonely bedsitter. I told him this and a few things about Hampstead, too, where I had once stayed for six months at what seemed like a permanent wine and cheese party.

'Write it, write it,' said Keith, which is what people say in the Street when they get a long answer to a simple question. It was certainly his idea that I should put it on paper and he was right. It was going to be a three part series: Hampstead, Chelsea and Mayfair, to run on a Monday, Tuesday and Wednesday and that was to be that; but then Louis Kirby, the editor of the paper, asked whether it could be extended and run weekly. At first I doubted whether it could. Hampstead, Mayfair and Chelsea were geographically some distance apart, but when I crossed the Hyde Park roundabout from Mayfair into Belgravia would there really be a perceptible differ- ence in just about one hundred yards? Indeed there was, and a similar difference was visible all over London in adjacent communities, between Putney and Barnes, Chelsea and Fulham, Islington and Hackney. Lou encour- aged me to find out. It is due to him that the series received such an extended run—five months, broken only by Christmas.

It quickly became apparent that the vitality of the idea lay in this sort of impossible truth. One street could make a difference, but a hundred years might not. All talk of shifting real estate values, up-and-coming neighbour- hoods and those which had seen their prime, paled beside certain permanent obsessions: Clapham is still genteel, Sydenham has always been overwhelmed by its own history, there has always been the touch of the *bar sinister* about Pimlico, the rake about Mayfair. Any Londoner understands these things by osmosis, and I have lived in London most of my life. I started in the south-east, then moved to the south-west as a child, then gradually north- east and back again to the south and the centre. Judging by other people's experience I have moved around a lot and lived in many different areas before finding a home. I moved about a lot abroad too and spent a good deal of time simply walking around cities like New York, where the transitions from one district to the next are particularly abrupt. Another editor, Jeff Miller of *Los Angeles Magazine*, got me hooked a long time ago on the ethnic divisions of Los Angeles, which I wrote about at length for him.

Ethnic groups have always clustered round certain parts of a city for good historical reasons. If that could happen, clearly there had to be reasons—less colourful perhaps and therefore more difficult to penetrate—whereby differ- ent sorts of English people came together in different neighbourhoods. Why they stayed together is a matter of choice, and this book is above all about the middle classes who have that choice. Whatever reasons we give for living in one place or another are not always the most essential ones. They are instinctive. People say that property is cheap and that they expect it to increase in value—but that is true of many areas; they say that the schools are good or that the shopping is marvellous; they praise the parks or the churches or the transport, and, according to what they choose, you have some idea of their priorities—or the priorities they expect you to expect. But when all is said and done it is a sense of identity we are all searching for in a like-minded community that doesn't question our peace of mind. Sometimes this means a virile life of church socials or Sunday morning cocktail parties, sometimes it is the privilege of being totally anonymous among the transient or the self-centred. Everyone knows when they feel out of water and when they have found the perfect environment.

That's people for you and the only distinction I want to make is that we are all different as well as the same, and this makes the world a very interesting place. Judging from the reactions of *Standard* readers, we perceive our neighbours' differences with a malicious kind of joy and feel deeply aggrieved when they perceive ours. We had a huge mailbag as a result of the *Standard* articles, and I spent many hours answering writers gloating over their own stripped pine and deprecating the same thing next door. Some people accused me of inaccuracies. Well, it would be remarkable if every reader fitted neatly into one pigeonhole. Most people recognise a bit of Hampstead and Barnes in them while they are at home in Richmond. But the fact is there are enough similarities to make it well worth commenting upon. The *Standard* series was called 'The London Sets' but the title *Metropolitan Myths* has an added truth. These are myths not gospel. Myths are built up over the years and are about feelings and ideas as well as facts.

If ever I had any doubt about the validity of the pieces it was allayed by the letters. All I had written was justified over and over again. Readers would niggle over my observations in the very terms that they were observed. When I said everybody in St John's Wood aims to look like Barbra Streisand or Neil Diamond, one lady wrote indignantly saying that she certainly didn't look like Ms Streisand, she only wished she did. From Notting Hill, where I wrote that they were violent and unlettered though they knew how to use a telephone, no one wrote. They telephoned instead. 'Are you the cow that wrote we were so violent?' they asked the Features secretary, Jackie Poole. 'Tell the cow we are going to come and thump 'er for writing about us.' Jackie's sense of humour deserves a special mention. Victoria Petrie-Hay must be very specially thanked for seeing it as a book: by the way, she loved every chapter except for the one on her particular area, which she thought quite unfair.

It has been great fun for everybody, and its long run as a series first proved this. Making predictions about people is something we all do every day of our lives. On a crowded bus we speculate what jobs other passengers do and where they will get off and we are more often right than wrong. I hope you will enjoy the opportunity to match my speculations against your own now the pieces are in book form.

Glenys Roberts
June 1982

METROPOLITAN MYTHS

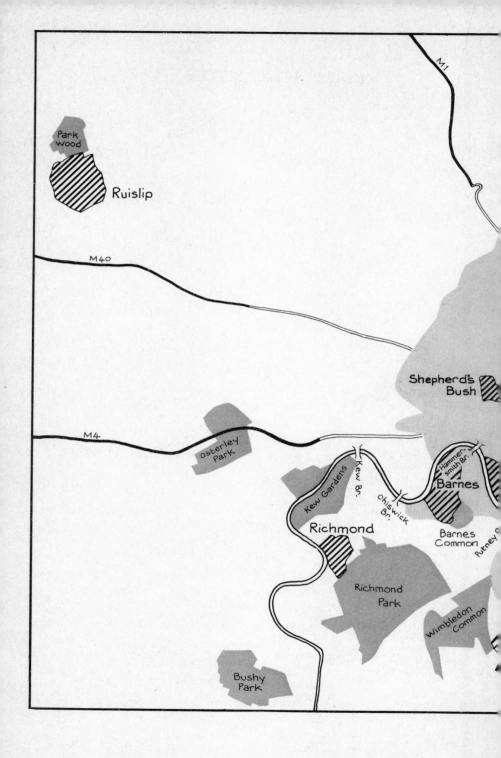

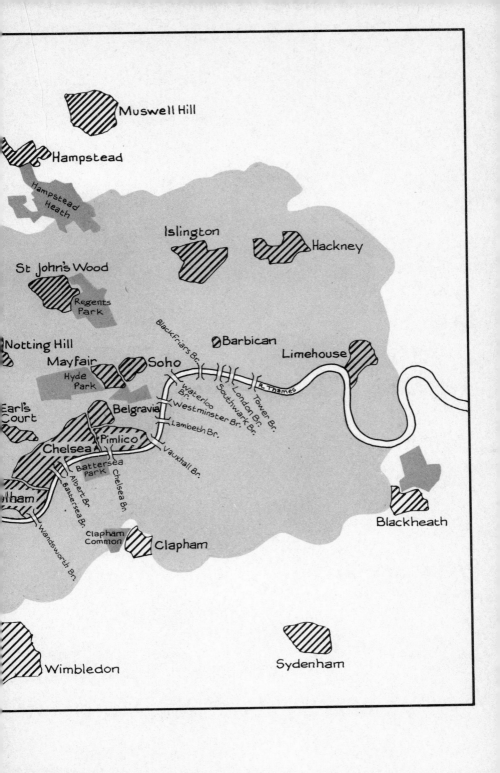

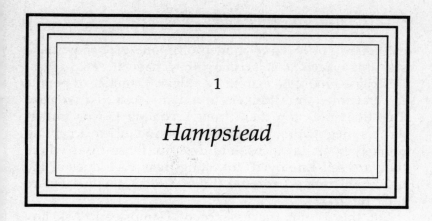

1

Hampstead

HAMPSTEAD RESIDENTS are possibly the most loyal of all Londoners to the place they choose to live. Their whole identity depends on being Hampstead Types and they scrimp and save in early life to buy any property which could loosely be described as anywhere near the Heath. This does not necessarily mean that it is actually near the Heath. Spiritual Hampstead extends from Kilburn in the west to Hackney in the east; from Barnet in the north to King's Cross in the south—but the nearer Hampstead people can get to the Royal Free Hospital the better. In later life this attitude certainly does Hampstead dwellers no harm at all. The bottom is as likely to drop out of Hampstead real estate as out of the air we breathe. Hampstead is the original up-and-coming place which came up as the meritocracy took over from the free spirits of the past. A house which was worth five thousand pounds twenty years ago is worth over a hundred and fifty thousand today. People who are just paying off their mortgages are doing so at the interesting rate of under forty pounds a month.

But money itself is not the point. Hampstead people rarely talk about money except to say they haven't got any. This is not usually true. Hampstead people are extremely canny about money, and one way they make sure they keep it is to deny they have it. To suggest otherwise would be extremely vulgar. Hampstead people are craftsmen and thinkers to a man—and to a woman. This does not stop them from becoming Lloyds underwriters, negotiating phenomenal redundancies, accepting unlikely book advances, and even (in those cases where they are self-employed) investing their VAT dues at the maximum interest for the three months allowed before their return.

But this is not the essence of Hampstead. Ask any Hampstead dweller why he lives in the area he does and he will talk about the facilities and the community. Belgravia residents never talk about their 'community'. They talk about the personalities who happen to have a pied-à-terre there: Algie who is in international banking, or Jimmy who was last seen on his yacht in the South of France. They wouldn't be seen dead belonging to anything as common as a community and they would hate to rely on communal facilities, just as Hampstead residents wouldn't be seen dead banking on money, even if they do. Hampstead is in touch with more meaningful things.

A typical Hampstead resident these days will have lived there most of his London life, which is ever since he came down from some northern town via Oxford or Cambridge where he went on a state scholarship. He gravitated to Hampstead to his fantasies and to his friends, but chances are he could afford nothing nearer the hub of it in the first place than a bedsitter in East Finchley. When he married (the first girl he met at a first-year lecture or a human rights meeting in the JCR) her added salary as a freelance proof-reader enabled them to progress to a small flat. When their first depressing autobiographical novels were published simultaneously they moved out somewhere charming with a sub-post office and a village green only to find that it shut down at 5.45. Hampstead people, being very gregarious, pretty soon they found themselves longing for all those ageing students, street philosophers and un-hung painters wandering around from pub to café day and night. They missed all their contemporaries dropping in to discuss the proper position they should all take on some intensely personal issue which they would then lecture everyone else about on a freelance basis in the up-market Sunday press. They quickly signed a contract with the up-market Sunday press and moved back to pivotal Hampstead, just a smidgen north of the Royal Free. This is an area which is in perfect contact with the High Street and the Heath but unspoiled by the commercialism of the one or the isolation of the other. Recently they moved again, all of three streets away, wisely investing his Fleet Street redundancy money or the royalties from some potboiler about a topical personality, or both. All this satisfies both their sense of history and of being part of a pioneering liberal élite. North of this particular fief is too nouveau riche, south is not rich enough, though it may be adequately cosmopolitan. But on the lower reaches of the Heath the place takes on a jigsaw social aspect which is mirrored in the network of tortuous little streets whose only plan is their apparent spontaneity.

Just how spontaneous Hampstead people are is actually open to question. They are nowhere near as spontaneous as Earl's Court people, they are a good deal less spontaneous than Shepherd's Bush people, and they are only half as spontaneous as Chelsea people. Sooner or later, like everyone else, Hampstead people gravitate to pubs, and the pubs reflect the nature of their clientele. Hampstead pubs are not tarted-up pubs, they are scruffy pubs, and a lot of scruffy people in uniform—bulky, hand-knit, natural fibre sweaters—spill out onto Hampstead pavements downing a lot of draught beer. These are very serious people. They talk a lot, all at the same time, and they talk a lot about integrity. Integrity does not mean the same thing all over London. In some places it smacks of the amateur. In others integrity means boring, in others still it is a good reason for not doing something you really should do but do not dare. In some places it still means honesty. In Hampstead integrity is both an apology and a brag. Integrity is what qualifies Hampstead residents to live in Hampstead.

Hampstead looks down on the rest of London from a great height. One of the best reasons for living on this high-priced piece of high ground is the magnificent panorama which its uppermost residents enjoy from the haughty heights of their roofs, attics, loft conversions and other pretentious exploitations of local planning permission. On a clear day they can see all of the rest of London strung out beneath them along the vacillating line of the River Thames. They look down on all the symbols of power: St Paul's, the NatWest skyscraper and the Post Office Tower. Hampstead residents say that the air is clearer in their neck of the woods, but they are not only thinking about their health. Neither are they thinking about their vision, though they may be thinking about their perspicacity. Hampstead people do not like to be down on the flats, rubbing shoulders with the blinkered and struggling masses. They like to keep their distance, to observe and to comment. Hampstead is full of commentators and satirists. You will come across the odd bona fide actor, musician, painter or playwright, but on the whole Hampstead people do not live so much by the arts as on the fringe of them. They are critics and surveyors of life and they work for newspapers and television. They write in respectable papers and pen solid books and they are genuinely, stolidly concerned with the future of society to which they feel they can make a good deal of difference.

Unlike Chelsea, where you may still come across genuine loonies dedicated to *la vie de bohème*, there is something reputable and middle-class about Hampstead which takes precedence over free-wheeling initiative. On the whole its residents are afraid of the avant-garde and attracted by the more easily assimilated values of the past.

Hampstead is full of conservationists. Hampstead people are so conservative that they have tried hard to be the only remaining area in London, if not in the whole country, without a McDonald's hamburger outlet. Their 'Burger Off!' campaign was typical Hampstead. It was very clever and not very self-serving. McDonald's is cheap, and so are Hampstead residents. They don't splash out at expensive eateries if they can help it and certainly not when they are picking up the check. 'Pretentious and over-priced,' they call their worthy local, Keats. They are, however, quite happy to be taken there by visiting American television executives buying obscure BBC2 series for American public broadcasting channels which nobody much watches. These series are usually made by people who live in Hampstead and watched by other people who live in Hampstead in the privacy of their television rooms. Hampstead people find it unthinkable to have a television in their living room, though they will almost certainly have a stereo with professional speakers, a cassette deck and an amplifier big enough to fill Bayreuth. Hampstead televisions, on the other hand, have a room of their own. This is not a measure of the awe in which they are held, but a measure of the contempt. Television would be a dirty word in Hampstead if so many Hampstead people did not make their living from it. Herein lies a knotty modern philosophical dilemma which accounts for a great deal of Hampstead angst. Some of the best state-educated brains in the country are at pains to reconcile this one: if much of television is demonstrably idle junk, how can so many worthy people be employed in the making of it? Only Hampstead people know the answer. They will tell you it whether you like it or not.

Recently things have been somewhat eased by the advent of video. Video is okay because (a) it is pioneering, (b) it is expensive, (c) they can collect a library full of their own works, and (d) it endows the square-eyed audience with an added dimension of free will. If you are watching television, your taste (or the lack of it) is more or less immediately discernible. If it is eight o'clock, chances are it's sit-com. If it's Wednesday it must be *Sportsnight*. But with a video machine no one can actually pin you down from a mere glance at the daily paper. On video you might be taking in a little educational Kiri Te Kanawa whatever time of day it is, or a late-night discussion of politics or art recorded in your absence while you were addressing a post-graduate audience on the use of the obscenity in the modern novel. Perhaps you are conducting a meaningful sex seminar with a group of like-minded friends committed to the critical analysis of the social function of erotic fulfilment by alternative means. Good grief, you wouldn't simply be watching the box because you had nothing better to do. At the very least Hampstead people watch because they are preparing an in-depth review for some erudite, obscure, small-circulation journal which is about to go out of business.

Hampstead people still read. They keep such a lot of books in the house that they are always putting up do-it-yourself bookshelves on the landings and in the loo. Best of all they like works of reference, dictionaries and manuals of instruction including how to put up do-it-yourself bookshelves. This means that Hampstead men are very handy around the house. They can change fuses and wire up whole tape decks, and pronounce with incontrovertible authority on partition walls and RSJs.

Hampstead men love gadgets and labour-saving devices and they always have the right tool for the job. They can mix a drink, boil a kettle and will even bring their wives and mistresses a cup of tea in bed. They are not very good at washing up but on the whole they are better than their wives, who mistrust labour-saving devices because they are afraid of being made redundant. This does not mean they do the washing up themselves. Hampstead wives are in the muddled grip of that familiar curse of the mid-twentieth century, rampant feminism. Rampant feminism means that the female of the species must never be seen to be doing anything she might reasonably be expected to do.

The Hampstead housewife is one of the worst house-wives and cooks in London. No doubt there are many Hampstead housewives and cooks who will contradict this but they haven't asked me to dinner lately. Despite her many cookbooks, displayed all over the kitchen on shelves erected by the man of the house, the Hampstead wife can scarcely knock together a meal at all. Often she is too busy orchestrating the conversation of her menfolk. Sometimes she is too busy drinking them under the table. Sometimes she is on a macrobiotic diet and doesn't drink at all. Any which way she hates cooking, though as an all-round person she prides herself on being able to do anything as well as the next person. If she is going to be in the kitchen, the fact is she is going to be seen to be in the kitchen, which is why she has persuaded her man to make the whole of the ground floor of their Victorian house into an open plan for living, just like everyone else in the street. Just like everyone else she puts in the obligatory stripped pine, the melancholy house-plants and the same glass furniture with chrome and cane trimmings. Then she asks the neighbours over to tell them how cheaply she has managed to have an expensive job done. At the same time

she will tell them how she is hiring the expensive video
and setting it off against expenses.

No one in Hampstead has any discreet skills. This is the
part of London where the hostess is most likely to
suddenly start breastfeeding her infant at a dinner party,
even though the infant may be three years old. Non-
Hampstead people are quite embarrassed by this ostentatious demonstration of nature in the raw. They are
sometimes apt to think that feeding time should be an
intimate personal moment for mother and child to share in
the peace of the nursery, but the Hampstead mother
knows this is a coy and dishonest approach. She knows
that it is a mark of intellect to vaunt her most primitive
assets. It is a way of disowning them. And it beats the hell
out of sterilising bottles.

The fact is Hampstead people don't really like children.
They certainly don't want to be inconvenienced by them.
They park them under the table in carry-cots and pretend
that nothing at all has changed since they decided to
become parents. This is always the subject of pre-plan-
ning. Hampstead people like to take a vote on it with their
friends and neighbours as well as partners. And if they are
not so keen on the end result, they love the mechanics of
reproduction—of emission, conception and parturition
(and whether or not this takes place lying down, standing
up, underwater and what to do about squatters' rights at
the Royal Free). No Hampstead children, be they ever so
young, are ignorant of the facts of life or the most
unattractive aspects of infidelity or divorce. They know all
about Valium, hysterectomy and VD. A daughter gets her
first Pill at thirteen and at sixteen her inter-uterine device.
Hampstead people allow their children to listen to adult
conversations and do as adults do; they simply pretend
that they are small versions of themselves. Some Hampstead parents allow their children to call them by their first

names. Hampstead children are forced to grow up at an early age, which accounts for a high instance of nervous breakdown later.

Hampstead parents cannot see this even when it happens to them. This is because they are above all theorists. They send their children to free schools because they like the theory of state education. They also like the theory of co-education. They believe in all theories of equality and cannot be persuaded from their theories even when they are contradicted by the facts. If their girl-children start cuddling babies they deplore this as a demonstration of role-playing which must have been brought into the house by some undesirable outside influence. If their offspring fail their exams, drop out and start peddling dope on the paper-round this is not the fault of the home or the school, but of society as a whole and as such a subject less of a jolly good spanking than of a jolly good thesis. Hampstead people are more tolerant of any theory than of any fact. They are invariably left-wing though they are rarely very politically active—even when they are in politics—because they are bystanders. They have no prejudices at all except those which they can support by the tortuous application of the conscious mind.

Hampstead people make these prejudices very plain indeed. They are very evangelical though they would not like to be thought of in the usual context of that word because they are atheists. They would also not like to be thought of as bullies, but bullies is what they are. If they are not preaching the virtues of jogging they are bound to be preaching the evils of smoking. Hampstead people are quite likely to order other people out of the room for smoking, and not necessarily their own room. It is as impossible for people to live and let die in Hampstead as it is impossible for their visitors to find an ashtray. No one in Hampstead ever produces an ashtray unasked, which accounts for the almost universal sight of a lot of cigarette butts stubbed out in the remains of a cheese or pâté salad. Hampstead people do not seem to mind this revolting sight. They distrust aesthetics because they are not intellectual, and cleanliness because it is bourgeois.

If Hampstead hospitality is offhand, Hampstead wine is plentiful. It flows and it flows, but it does not very often flow from the domains of Baron de Rothschild, for example. Hampstead people mistrust luxury even when they can afford it. Luxury is called selling-out. Hampstead people buy their wine from cut-price places in Soho. It usually comes from Algeria and it gives you a hangover before you have finished one glass. Other people refer to it as sheep-dip or paint-stripper, but the quality of the taste is not as important as the quality of the conversation it provokes.

On the whole Hampstead people regard good taste of any kind with the utmost suspicion. They feel more comfortable with bad taste, especially when it comes to clothes. In some cases this casual approach amounts to a cult which is so powerful that even when Hampstead people want to dress right they somehow get it wrong. Porridge open-weave jackets, lime green or shetland crofter shirts with Oriental ties are the delight of snazzy Hampstead dressers. For, while being deeply involved in the cultural life of our capital city, they have never lost touch with the sod. Their style of dressing indicates this. It is backward. Hampstead people have country cottages in backward places with no central heating, running water or electricity. They visit them continually, and even like to do so in midwinter. They like nothing more stimulating than to be stranded in a snow drift in deepest Wales or in wildest Northumbria, delivering lambs with their bare hands from stranded ewes. This demonstrates their initiative.

If a Hampstead person has a home abroad he will invariably have it in the Dordogne, a very over-rated part of France which looks just like England, and feels it. The sun almost never shines, which accounts for the emerald green of the grass, yet Hampstead people can be found in tribes shivering by the banks of swollen rivers, drinking cold red plonk and going to market wellie-deep in mud remarking how unusual the weather is for the time of year. There is no hardship they will not endure. They draw water from the far-away well, sleep with spiders and chop wood. To stray anywhere near an acknowledged actual pleasure centre would be considered deeply decadent. Their idea of a 'different' holiday is to borrow someone else's uncomfortable house in another uncomfortable part of the world. If they go on a business trip, Hampstead people stay with colleagues, not in hotels. If they fly, they fly stand-by or, cheaper still, bucket-shop. Their idea of a successful business trip is to change their economy ticket for a walk-on fare. Hampstead people never fly first class and could never accept a free holiday on the Riviera. They prefer to go for long walks in green anoraks carrying plastic bags full of wheatgerm sandwiches rather than disport themselves in any comfortable watering spot with a rum punch in one hand and their eye on a teenage nymphet.

Yet the fact is that, while capable of the most incomprehensible puritanism, they are also given to the most dangerous, extreme and overt extra-marital dalliances. These are naturally performed not for the pleasure of the flesh but the good of the mind. This makes them thoroughly excusable. Hampstead people mark their bed-partners according to their Mensa-rating rather than for their nutcracker thighs or hairy chests. Most of Hampstead has at some time or other had carnal knowledge of the rest of Hampstead. Their ratings on a scale of 1–100 are public knowledge and largely dependent on the public positions of influence they occupy. Anyone who loses his public position is unlikely to see much action between the sheets. Anyone who hangs on to it is excused any amount of philandering, which is almost always heterosexual. In case there should be any confusion about the source of the attraction, Hampstead people have quite different sex symbols than people in any other part of London. Glasses are considered irresistible, hair is worn slightly dank and completely natural, fringes are encouraged to cover the best features, bras are discouraged and so is make-up, face-lifts would be unthinkable, acne is preferable, chewed fingernails desirable, and no one is ever in any doubt as to who is pregnant, menstruating and suffering from breast cancer.

In other words all those brave forms of artifice which carry most people through life are deeply frowned upon in this particular part of north London. If Hampstead people were not so happy living in Hampstead, they would be quite happy in Greenwich Village. Hampstead people are a lot like New Yorkers. They are neurotic and stoical to a degree and quite content to queue in the rain to see Woody Allen's latest film. I am not sure that they have a sense of humour, so I do not expect them to believe that some of my best friends live in Hampstead.

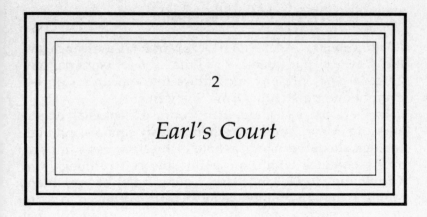

2

Earl's Court

EARL'S COURT IS the first part of London proper you hit
when you come in from the airport, but it is by no means
any sort of advertisement for it.

Cheap hotels and grotesque boarding houses, give-
away newspapers and give-away sex, takeaway pizza,
takeaway kebab, takeaway noodles and curry and chips,
takeaway hamburger, sharma and fish; fast food and
overnight graffiti and transient people of all persuasions;
more Australians than on Bondi Beach, more Arabs than
in the London Clinic, more Sri Lankans than in Safeways,
more drunks than in Langan's Brasserie, more genteel
poverty than in the home for retired gentlefolk, more spies
than in Cambridge, more Filipinos than are known to the
Home Office, more pushers than in Penang, more flashers
than in Twickenham, more mud than in Hamburg, more
pansies than in Kew Gardens; more leather freaks,
bondage freaks, S & M freaks, rubber freaks, foot-
fetishists, hand-jobs and hangers-out, drop-outs and
drug-addicts, coprophiliacs and necrophiliacs, clones,
fags, poofs, gays, homos, machos, queers, poofters
and pederasts, dames and lesbians, drag artists and
down-and-outs, winos, weirdos, bums and butches, tarts,
transsexuals and transvestites than in the Swiss Alps,

Johannesburg, Copenhagen, Amsterdam, Casablanca and the Bowery put together. Quite a few perverts too. Queens past, present and future live in Earl's Court— even at one time Lady Diana Spencer.

Earl's Court is cosmopolitan, confused, colonial, crapulous and classy. Time was when its leafy squares and high ceilings sheltered many people of the Princess's impeccable bloodlines within an aristocratic belt running from The Boltons to Holland Park. Young ladies of prominent families, though prohibitive means, are overjoyed to share flats with such a noble address and such an educational outlook. Their mothers sleep in peace in Scotland, secure in the knowledge that Fiona and Caroline are safe in (or near) SWs 3, 7 and 10, while waiting for their Prince to come. He's more likely to be a merchant banker. Scotland is best left only once a year, for Christmas shopping in Knightsbridge or Sloane Square, and Mother is never ever mildly surprised by Earl's Court since she always approaches it from the town side by taxi.

Time was when it was safe to travel by tube to Earl's Court even at midnight. Not today. Earl's Court is a bordello, a latrine, a rubbish bin and a hunting ground. Earl's Court is rarely safe at midday. No one in their right mind lives there and quite a few people do who aren't.

All this would be tragic if Earl's Court people did not live there because they liked it. They like it precisely because it is so shiftless that they cannot be pinned down. They like it because it sings of youth even when they are past middle age. They like it because it is temporary and uncommitted and adventurous and unashamed. They like it because there is the suggestion of moving on, or having moved. This is the part of London people instinctively head for in the middle of a push-bike tour of the world or on their way overland, on foot, from Alaska to Tasmania.

Earl's Court people have dormobiles rather than cars so they are never dependent on any one place. They send each other postcards from all the other vile places on the globe and collect used stamps and dog-eared bits of paper currency to remind themselves of their travels. They collect hippy scarves and ethnic habits and children of varying hues. They collect indigestion and ulcers and abortions, but in the midst of the most vicious vortex they remind themselves that they are free.

Yet in spite of all their gregarious habits—importuning people on the streets, touching them up in singles' pubs and soliciting in telephone booths—Earl's Court people are loners. They may share arctic bathrooms and greasy kitchens with other Earl's Court dwellers, they may queue up in gangs for pay telephones in peeling halls, but home is likely to be a single bedroom with a damp patch in the corner, a sagging ceiling, a bed saturated with brief joy and, rather than a live-in lover, a couple of rats for companionship attracted by the mouldering contents of an old baked bean tin. Australians, Scotsmen and German au pairs are delighted with this sort of thing. But, unlike Chelsea (where everyone claims to live with an address anywhere between Fulham and Victoria), or Clapham (where everyone claims to live with an address anywhere between Vauxhall and Brighton), half of Earl's Court never admits to living in Earl's Court these days. Other people describe it variously as The Boltons, Brompton Road, Lower Knightsbridge, Kensington and Chelsea, Stamford Bridge, just off the King's Road or Near Rassell's. But all these places are actually situated at more or less safe distance from that hub of evil enterprise, that part of the Earl's Court Road which runs like a tawdrier 42nd Street between the arterial thoroughfare of the Cromwell Road and the foolish philanderings of Coleherne Corner.

Earl's Court pubs are not nice quiet meeting places with

a turquoise patterned carpet on the floor, naughty red lampshades overhead and hot Cornish pasties and Babycham on the counter. Earl's Court pubs are less naughty than nauseating. Earl's Court pubs have brown lino underfoot and fag ends, and juke boxes and snooker tables in the corners and space invader machines to play with if you're scraping the barrel and can't find anyone to pick up. They are very big and very noisy and if they are not full of loitering leather queens wearing their keyrings on their belt loops and flaunting handkerchiefs according to their sexual preferences, they are full of cussing colonials knocking back the beer out of quart mugs which display vulgar inscriptions about their capacities. When they have finished knocking back the beer they fall round the corner to swallow a yodelling sausage or a hot diggity.

Compared to the tedious life of Winnipeg, Durban or Down Under, Earl's Court is obviously paradise indeed. You are allowed to get drunker than in Melbourne, Wagga Wagga or the whole of the Northern Territory. What is expected of Les Patterson on an evening out in Sydney is but a drop in the ocean in Kangaroo Valley, as the Aussies affectionately call it. The Fosters flows and so do the after-effects. In Earl's Court you measure how good a time you are having by how sick you can get at someone else's expense and how often you have to take yourself off for relief against the wall of someone else's mews cottage. Some people in Earl's Court are literally legless all the time, and one inhabitant has solved his problem by propelling himself along in a wheelchair with one hand while supporting a bottle of cooking sherry with the other.

Even the Arabs, who are not supposed to drink at all for the love of Allah, do so in Earl's Court. This is not surprising because Arabs in Earl's Court are pretty much out on a gangrened limb. It combines the squalor of the souk with an inhospitality they have never been used to. It is not much fun existing in some down-at-the-heel frigid London suburb when you come from the desert where the heat sterilises the detritus and you are among family, never mind friends.

Arabs in Earl's Court are lonely like everyone else, but Arabs don't like being lonely. What is more, they are often on their last legs just waiting around to be admitted to some overpriced London nursing home to have themselves nipped, tucked and cleaned out by all those British doctors who have abandoned the National Health Service to the Pakistanis. Richer Arabs wait around for their final operations in Mayfair or Baker Street or Bayswater, but the monolingual middle classes have to make do with Earl's Court, which puts up its prices to celebrate the occasion. Earl's Court Arabs wander coldly from cut-price chemist to cut-price souk eating takeaway meat balls with sodden French fries and being propositioned by under-age girls from the Southern Hemisphere or Northern Europe who think everyone wearing a djellabah and a headdress owns an oil well and is a sex maniac. This is because it is not easy to tell the social status of an Arab unless you can get a good look at his feet peeking out from underneath his gown. Rich Arabs wear Gucci slippers while poor ones wear filthy tennis shoes. People who proposition Arabs in Earl's Court are wasting their time. They should move up town and join the steroid set. Age does not wither these hopeful members of the male sex, nor custom stale the infinite variety of their requests. Steroid treatment in Mayfair is the equivalent of heart pills and eye-drops in Earl's Court. There is only one problem for the would-be escort of the sexually restored sheik: he is much harder to meet than the street Arab of the Earl's Court Road since he is usually closeted behind net curtains in Park Lane making the most of his rejuvenation before his prescription runs out.

Earl's Court has very many chemists, which makes life simple for a lot of drug addicts. What with the welfare office on the one hand and the chemist on the other it is hard to imagine a simpler way of life. Earl's Court streets are heavily trod between the counter where they hand out the social security and the counter where they hand out the methadone. Naturally enough, Earl's Court has a lot of doctors who operate behind such grimy façades that even if they do not deserve to be struck off the register it certainly looks that way. Earl's Court has a lot of dentists and opticians which suggests that Earl's Court people not only have rotten teeth from all the fast food, but failing eye-sight as well. This is because there are a lot of retired and elderly Earl's Court residents, who may be on their uppers but always shop at Harrods. Retired gentlefolk still cluster in the once grand mansion blocks, which they refuse to renovate in the forlorn hope that the landlord will recognise their worthiness and gentility. Retired diplomats and tea-planters make a beeline for Earl's Court when they come home because they have been abroad so long they can conceivably claim not to know anything of its changed reputation. They can be seen wearing be-mused looks and regimental ties walking small dogs to and from the cut-price off-licence for the next half bottle of gin and dodging the meths drinkers. They form residents' associations of like-minded misfits and write scandalised letters to the newspapers but they never move out of the district, partly because of the inadequacy of their pensions and partly because with all its echoes of the far-flung reaches of empire they actually do feel at home there. Earl's Court recalls the slums of Bangkok, Calcutta and Singapore rolled into one. It makes Soho, the acknow-ledged sin centre of London, look rather like Welwyn Garden City.

In Earl's Court they don't just sweep the rubbish under

the carpets, they sweep the rubbish under the bushes in the front gardens, and the back. They don't even bother to put it into black plastic bags. Even if they did so no one would take it away. In contrast to all the 'nice' suburbs of London like Richmond, Clapham and Barnes, keeping up with the Joneses in Earl's Court means being more scruffy than they are. It means living in a house with less paint and letting the garden look like a bomb site. There is a suggestion, amidst all this squalor, of being blooded by the world, of keeping alive the rebellious spirit of individuality which is so much more precious than clean conformism. The proudest spirits of Earl's Court are conscious of floating on the top of the septic tank, looking forward to the day when their courage will be rewarded by the installation of mains sewerage.

Earl's Court is in a constant state of alert against the bourgeoisie. Where people in Clapham sweep up their leaves and clip their hedges, prune their roses, pull up their dandelions and mend their garden gates, people in Earl's Court understand that a full life is liable to include rack and ruin. Cars depreciate before you drive them out of the garage. Whereas people in East Sheen have their washing on the line by eight a.m. and polish their cars before lunch, people in Earl's Court stay in bed until it is too dark to do anything virtuous. Whereas Putney people put on their overcoats over their nightdresses to take in the milk, Earl's Court people put them on over their nightdresses to go to the off-licence. They are proud to live in the big city, albeit on the edge of it, with all the attendant seaminess, noise and reality. They have only one thing in common with suburban people and that is their dogs. Dogs are a way of attracting attention to their owners and attracting attention is what Earl's Court people are about as well as everyone else.

Earl's Court people, however, like their rendezvous

with others to be brief. Apart from the pub, the off-licence, the station, the mini-market, the telephone booth, the stained fast-food counter and the unswept takeaway, the hub of Earl's Court social life is the launderette. This is a very good place to meet people between the soap cycle and the hot rinse. Earl's Court people can be found in the launderette in their legions late at night wondering whether the guy with the lavender longjohns in the cool wash has more bars to his electric fire, enough small change for the gas meter or a spare roll-your-own in his American army surplus raincoat pocket. The trouble is that Earl's Court launderettes are so soiled that the clothes come out even dirtier than they went in.

Pride in their own condition and prejudice against everyone else's are the two tenets of everyone's creed. Earl's Courters are no different in this either. If all else fails they will simply move on. Meanwhile they will plumb the depths of their own peculiar culture and enjoy attracting the pity of passers-by. They may even attact stares of envy and a frisson of admiration for the freelance life elevated to a high art form. Yet, far from the exotic intent, Earl's Court finally reduces everything to the banal. There is no mystery at all left in Earl's Court. Earl's Court people have managed to take the X out of sex as they have managed to take the taste out of food and the intricacy out of the community. What you see in Earl's Court is what you can have. Once they have had it Earl's Court people never shape up, they simply ship out, to the grave or another transit camp.

3

Clapham

CLAPHAM IS A very long way from London, but try saying this to those people who live there. They will rave about their delightful little bijou residences just the other side of Chelsea Bridge, so convenient and so cheap and so up-and-coming and what's more only five minutes away from anywhere they want to be. This is probably true as long as they don't want to be anywhere else but Clapham. It is probably true as long as they do all their moving around between the hours of midnight and first light. Just try visiting them any other time and you will certainly get stuck in a traffic jam somewhere around Sloane Square, on top of Chelsea Bridge or underneath the railway lines in Battersea. In winter you will get lost in the fog on the common, at all times you will get lost in the one-way system around it, which like all other one-way systems suffers from schizophrenia and has an annual change of mind.

Clapham people won't have any of this. Whereas Hampstead people are proud of the fact that Hampstead is out on a limb, Clapham people just deny it. Clapham is convenient yet countrified. Clapham people are cultured and classy.

Clapham is not entirely common. Clapham people are

respectable. They are so respectable that people who don't
live in Clapham at all are apt to say that they do. People
who live in Wandsworth Common or South Battersea,
people who live in Tooting and Balham, people who live
in Nine Elms, Vauxhall, Stockwell and Lavender Hill, all
lay claim to Clapham. Almost everybody who lives anywhere at all south of the river says they live in Clapham,
including some who live halfway to Brighton. People who
live in Clapham Junction say they live in Clapham, but
Clapham people proper know this is not so. Clapham
people live in 'convenient' mansion flats and draughty
Victorian mansions nowhere near any actual facilities like
a station. They also live in an exclusive ghetto of identical
tiny little houses on the west side.

Whole generations of typical young married couples
have been persuaded by typical thrusting magniloquent
estate agents to find themselves typical attractively-priced
Edwardian terraced properties with typical possibilities for
improvement, which means gutting the house and putting a brass knocker on it. Very often these desirable little
residences are bought for them by the father and mother
of one half of the couple, usually the wife, so they can start
their married life a safe distance away from the family on
whom they might otherwise continue to depend. Father
and mother rarely live anywhere near Clapham themselves but think of it as a good investment which will be a
nest egg, a pension fund and something in the kitty for a
rainy day. Since father and mother have to have a little
spare cash to think in this way they are privileged and
therefore assumed to belong to the upper classes—hence
the process of encouraging fledgling brides to make the
most of workers' cottages is known as the 'gentrification'
of Clapham. The properties may indeed come up somewhat with coaxing, but nothing much else does in
Clapham.

Clapham is cosy. It is so cosy Walt Disney would have been proud of it. It is quaint and contrived and entirely predictable. Clapham people have 2.1 children (planned), 2.1 animals (strays) and 2.1 cars (brand new). They are consumers. They are first to read the ads, first to believe them, first indeed to write them and first to place their order for the new Mini Metro, the folding bicycle, the all-in holiday in Portugal or the Sunday supplement duvet coat offer—such good value.

Clapham people are uniform. This is because they work in the law (where they have to wear pinstripes), in radio (where they have to wear beards), in television (where they have to wear Hush Puppies) and in advertising (where they have to wear jeans). Clapham wives work in related professions to Clapham husbands. They earn two vast salaries per family which means they feel entitled to spend them. Once they have revamped the house and put in the Victorian drawing room, the Edwardian bathroom, the art nouveau bedroom, the *House and Garden* kitchen, the clever conservatory, the extra bedroom, the useful annexe, the Habitat study, the attic playroom, the patio suntrap and the Sissinghurst garden, they have lots and lots of money left over to fill all this with useless ephemera acquired at great cost with very little resale value. They collect old matchbox labels and interesting tea-caddies and curious cache-pots and old clothes and paper lampshades and rattan blinds and gloomy aspidistras and junk jewellery and sepia photographs of people who may or may not be their grandmothers. They collect books of limericks to read in the loo and etchings of the Inner Temple. They buy offer prints by hopeless artists and offer kitchen knives with prodigious capabilities and offer vacuum cleaners of the same ilk.

Clapham people are offer-crazy and gadget-minded. They give each other Sparklets for Christmas and cocktail-

shakers and the sort of hypodermic bottle-openers used
by Bulgarian agents to murder ostentatious dissidents.
Clapham people open a lot of bottles. They enjoy their
drinking habits and they are connoisseurs when it comes
to them. They don't fool around with any old thing that
purports to be alcohol. They believe in named brands, as
long as they have read the name in some magazine. They'
order in their wine by the case and always make sure they
are first on the list for the new Beaujolais even if it is
utterly acid and undrinkable. Clapham people rave about
it. They keep it in offer wine racks under the stairs and call
this the cellar. This means the wine never runs out in
Clapham. It is easier to go to the cellar than the pub and
you can get a lot drunker a lot cheaper. This means that
Clapham days usually start with a stiff Bloody Mary after
the night before. Naturally some Clapham people drink
Perrier water but this is usually because they are after the
advertising account.

Clapham people entertain a lot because there is absolutely nothing else to do in Clapham. There is no night life
unless you make it, apart from the roller-disco where you
cannot be admitted unless you prove to the doorman that
you can speak nicely. But people who can speak nicely do
not want to go roller-skating, which is a down-market
pursuit even in gentrified Clapham. They want to stay at
home instead where they are extremely proud of their
standards of hospitality. Clapham people dress up for
their dinner parties and clean the house from top to
bottom. They clean up for the cleaning lady and have a
nervous breakdown if you spill wine on their offer
tablecloth. When they are not entertaining they are simply
not at home because they are being entertained. When
they are not being entertained they are asleep. This means
it is impossible ever to get anyone in Clapham on the
telephone.

On Sundays Clapham people dress up in nice wool frocks and tweed jackets with elbow patches and give lunch parties for other Clapham people who wear nice wool frocks and tweed jackets with elbow patches and ask them back to their place the Sunday after where they meet all the same guests, talk about all the same things, eat the same food and are confident they are more scintillating hosts than their neighbours. Clapham people are extremely competitive though not very adventurous. They shop, cook and decorate by mutual consent and pride themselves on their cleverness. They buy their Huskies in midsummer by mutual consent and their frocks at garage sales and their vegetables from street markets. This is called 'bargaining', whatever they pay. They claim to have the best butcher in London and the best delicatessen. They claim this is one of the reasons they live in Clapham. They call all their tradesmen by their first names, which is a sure sign of gentrification.

Clapham people are very adventurous in their modern kitchens. This is called 'being thrifty'. They can make soup out of anything at all, just as long as they have a Cuisenart or a Magimix or a Moulinex or a Chefette or a combination of all or any of these devices, including one on offer from a Sunday supplement, of course. Clapham cooks are not earth mothers who believe in roughage and nuts like people north of the Park. Clapham cooks are labour-saving and practical. They are convenience cooks and their definition of a good dinner party is to let the food take care of itself. Whereas Hampstead people feel guilty just looking at a piece of machinery and would be happier doing their laundry down at the river, Clapham people are lost more than a foot away from an electric socket. They deplore people who do not have electric blenders and electric carving knives and electric can-openers, or better still multi-purpose machines which can perform all these functions simultaneously. There are a lot of these machines in Clapham, and a lot of coffee-grinders and orange-squeezers and spit-kits and toasters and double-boilers and pressure-cookers and infra-red grills and micro-wave ovens. Unfortunately this does not always improve the quality of the food. Clapham people will buy grouse because they are so gentrified and serve them up with oven chips. This is not a short cut, or even a piece of ignorance, but simply a handy hint. They are extremely offended if you do not recognise it as such or detect anything else bland about their cuisine. You won't get invited again if you reach for the pepper and salt; they think garlic anti-social and mustard and vinegar down-right common. People invited to eat in Clapham often go home as hungry as when they arrived. This is because lunch is served very late indeed and they may have to go home before it reaches the table. It is served late to allow plenty of time to study the operating manuals of all the labour-saving devices and to leave plenty of room for drinks, which is the real reason for gathering in the first place.

Drinks are not the same as wine, but they are just as important to Clapham people. After kicking off with the Bloody Mary the Clapham husband switches to the swizzle stick and at all times wears vinyl aprons with things like 'FASTEST BARMAN IN THE WORLD' written on them. This is not considered vulgar but humorously trendy. Every Clapham husband knows how to be the perfect housewife. He can knock up any recipe from any book written by Caroline Conran (in which case he will wear the apron with the butcher's stripes on it). He wears it to open the door to his guests just to show them who does what round here. While he is stacking the dishes in the dishwasher he wears an apron saying 'MOTHER'S LITTLE HELPER'. On the whole, the Clapham husband is happier in the kitchen than in the garden and he is happiest of all at the drinks' cupboard or on his way to the cellar. The Clapham garden is the province of the Clapham wife who has it paved over immediately on arrival. She also has the house re-pointed in scarlet and black and replaces the wooden gate with a wrought iron one, the privet hedge with chains and the name 'Mon Repos' with a number. She buys a lot of monstera plants and sweetheart vines to climb up the inside of the windows where the net curtains used to be. She puts passion flowers next to the front door where the previous residents had hydrangeas and roses and pyracantha sprawling all over the lime green stucco.

It is by no means essential to have children in Clapham, especially if you are a theatrical agent or an unpublished poet. But what with the good air and the trees and the icecream vans and the fact that one block away from the Victoriana on the common it is all on the scale of toyland, it is not a bad place to start a family. Children arrive two and a half years apart and go to the Montessori school as soon as they can walk. They wear clever clothes run up by clever seamstresses and go on holiday with their parents to condominiums in Spain or Italy or one of those modestly-priced ski resorts which are so far below the snow line the *après* begins after breakfast. This pleases Clapham fathers. Clapham people are very gregarious and cannot bear the idea of going on holiday on their own. They have misgivings about going with their neighbours, but they have many more misgivings about going by themselves. As everyone knows who has tried to go on holiday with their neighbours, good relations rarely last beyond the aeroplane ride. What with the fine calculations as to who should pay for the taxi, the magazines, the drinks on board, whether or not you have forgotten to turn off the iron, will the cat be all right, should it be gin or whisky at the duty free and why is someone else's offspring's chewing-gum stuck in your hair, neighbouring parents are rarely talking to each other by the time they arrive at the villa which is not what it was cracked up to be and the beds are not aired. This means Clapham people have to go away with a different neighbour each year. Since Clapham people have an eye to value they plan their holidays ahead of time and pick on their different neighbours accordingly. This means that by the time August comes around they have probably fallen out with them anyway. They go on holiday together all the same and blame each other's children for ruining everything.

Everything in Clapham is done together, no matter what it is. You do not necessarily have to be married to live over the bridge, but if you are single you probably live with a lot of other single people. Clapham people do not like loners. They are suspicious of them. It is all very well to have affairs with married people (in fact in Clapham it is essential), but it is not all right to have affairs with singles. Affairs with singles lead to trouble. They lead to trouble even if you are single yourself because someone always wants to get married sooner rather than later. The answer to that is to give in, get married and have affairs with married people like everyone else. Clapham people have affairs with the people who live next door. They have twosomes and threesomes and foursomes, but they rarely run away from home for good because they cannot decide who should have custody of the stereo, the video and the dishwasher. Clapham people like frissons but they do not like upheavals, and they only like dramas when they are being played out among friends. Even when drama is their business it is liable to be on the tame side. Clapham actors have safe jobs at the National Theatre.

Clapham people are voyeurs who never feel completely safe off their own patch. They like small houses and small cars and small circles and they get agoraphobic both in the open country and the big city. The biggest thing in Clapham is the common, the meeting-place of natty joggers and Rastafarian karate experts. It is also the place where the alternative Miss World contest has been held, and sundry other peculiar raves. This sort of thing would be far too *outré* for other London suburbs, but it is not for nothing that Clapham people live right over the bridge from Chelsea. They would never live anywhere near the King's Road themselves for they are far too ostensibly respectable for that sort of thing. They would never wear red and green striped hair or swastikas tattooed on their wrists or multiple earrings in one ear rather than the other, but they enjoy watching people who do. They would never admit to being incestuous, incautious or bored. Neither would they admit to being moralistic and cautious. They like gossip at other people's expense and some of them even write it. They write gossip for small circulation magazines like *Ritz* and *New Style*, which may or may not have survived by the time you read this because they are so incestuous they are only ever read by their contributors. But deep down Clapham people are not all that frivolous. Some of them are ambitious enough to spend a good deal of their time working out how to leave the place. These Clapham people can be found cavorting in high-priced London restaurants until all hours of the morning waiting until the traffic has thinned out on the bridge so they really *can* get home in five minutes—as long as they don't mind the expense by taxi since they are invariably too drunk to drive.

Sooner or later smart people realise they should buy into Clapham as an investment and go to live some place else like Notting Hill. This is only what their in-laws, who bought the houses on their behalf, could have told them in the first place.

4

Mayfair

MAYFAIR IS AN extremely beautiful part of London, inscrutable on the whole to the rest of town but not necessarily invulnerable for all that. It has many protected buildings, lovely squares and unexpected mews backwaters, and at weekends it can be the quietest place in the city, except for the City itself—unless you live hard up against the American Embassy in Grosvenor Square where everybody in the world chooses to demonstrate on a Sunday, no matter what it is they are demonstrating about.

Those who live in Mayfair are adamant that, despite this apparent proximity to power, it should remain a residential area and not be sucked into some trashy town plan which fills the streets with junk businesses and the houses with offices. Those who don't live there are equally determined to storm the barricades of the tiny square mile, suspecting it of inflated privileges which should be redistributed. This makes Mayfair residents extremely defensive, and whether they are a duchess or the local tobacconist they are fiercely protective of their patch. Parvenus they may be, compared to Belgravia people— Mayfair has always had the aura of new enterprise—but they are the people who have given the place viability and

any attempt to supplant them by a new generation of
parvenus renders them insecure if not paranoid. Mayfair
people never answer the doorbell unless they are expecting a caller. Sometimes they still don't answer. They hate
surprises and they are very secretive.

It is hard work living in Mayfair and there is many a sad
story behind its grand façades. There is many a sad story
in front of its grand façades as the village gives way to the
carpet bazaar. Mayfair is fighting to survive. Mayfair
people are either deeply in debt or extremely flush. They
are deeply in debt one week and extremely flush the next.
They are gamblers and hustlers and, just like Mr
Micawber, they are always hoping something will turn
up. When it does they flaunt it. They have champagne on
their breakfast trays and drink Malvern water with their
whisky. When it doesn't they go without breakfast.

Mayfair people are deeply into money. They love what
it can buy, but more than that they love the money itself.
They love flashing it around and fingering it. They love
folding money – oncers, fivers, tenners, ponies, grands.
They carry wads of singles in their breast pockets to make
them bulge and offer fifty-pound notes to taxi drivers in
the hope they will waive the fare. They carry big notes in
money clips in their side pockets and leave their small
change on the dressing table so as not to spoil the line of
their suits. They pay their butlers off in fivers in the
middle of cocktail parties and they give their wives the
housekeeping in the middle of crowded restaurants, but
they never have the exact money and they always give
short change. Look after the pennies, they say, and the
pounds will look after themselves. Mayfair people hoard
their small change in cigar boxes. If they owe you money
they never have enough on them. They never write
cheques because their cheque books have just run out.
They never open envelopes with windows in them on

principle. They run up huge debts even when they could settle them because they are too insecure to pay. This means that they end up even more in debt.

Mayfair people talk a lot about cashflow, which means that the cash doesn't flow. They never pick up bar bills and they always smoke other people's cigarettes. Mayfair people never give up their vices, they simply find someone to pay for them. They are too devious to *ask* for a packet of cigarettes, but not to summon the Italian waiter and put it on the bill. When the time comes to pay, the Mayfair man has always forgotten to go to the bank that day. Or he seems to have just lost a fiver. Or he has left his American Express card in the pocket of his other suit.

Clothes mean money to people in Mayfair along with everything else, but they are not plumage as they are in Chelsea. In Mayfair clothes are bankability. Mayfair people wear their fur coats to go to the bank manager and to get their jewellery out of the pawn shop. Very few people in Mayfair own any real jewellery any more. They have the right accessories: they have the Cartier wedding ring—whether or not they are married—the Asprey's watch, the Gucci shoes and the Vuitton luggage. This means they can always get a good table at a restaurant and sign the bill. It also means that, since everyone has exactly the same accessories, they can never risk checking in their luggage. Mayfair people travel with a handbag and buy their clothes at the other end. Better still they borrow them. Mayfair people are not too proud to wear other people's clothes, but they must have the right designer label. Their coats must say Yves St Laurent and their suits Calvin Klein so they get the right respect from the hat-check girl. Some Mayfair people buy their jackets at Marks & Spencer's and sew old Cardin labels into them. This works very well and nobody seems to notice the difference. They rarely take their fur coats off in restaurants because they are never insured and so that everyone else can see them.

Mayfair people are all about labels, starting with the Mayfair address. A property in Mayfair is worth several in the Bush, so they cling to their bricks and mortar like snails to their shells. No matter that Bayswater is leafier, Knightsbridge has better shopping and Belgravia is more exclusive, Mayfair residents are home-loving to a fault. But the homes are not exactly what you might think. Just like the fur coats they are rarely insured. If they are insured they are often over-valued. Behind those strong defences there are very few Picassos. Spot a work of art in Mayfair and it is liable to be forged. Mayfair people employ home decorators who can turn out a Schiele or a Chagall or a Matisse at will. They are very plausible forgeries and they are often only detectable to the naked eye by the suspicious way they exactly match the drapes.

Mayfair people buy their status symbols by the yard. They buy books and never read them, they buy newspapers and never get beyond the share prices. They buy plants to fill the spaces where the Dresden figurines should be. They never buy them at Constance Spry, they get someone up at crack of dawn to do a deal down at Nine Elms instead. Mayfair people are always doing deals. They know people in clever places. They know doormen who know everything there is to know, and caretakers who will walk their dogs and feed their cats. There are cats in Mayfair by the score because Mayfair people are loners, or they are old, or they live in old buildings where they invariably have mice. They also have cockroaches and black beetles and silverfish and wiggly worms that come out at night. Mayfair people know this because they are very nocturnal.

A typical Mayfair resident lives in a bedsitter. He may have five floors, but what with the heating and the lighting and the price of servants these days he is unlikely to live on more than one of them. Whole families live in one room. In the rest of the house they have white carpets and chandeliers and extensions to the telephone in case their ship comes in, but no furniture meanwhile to speak of at all. They can't afford the heating and they can't afford the electric light. They wrap themselves in duvets and watch television in the dark and go to bed, though not to sleep, with the *Nine O'Clock News*. If the television breaks down they are in real trouble. Nobody in Mayfair can afford to get anything mended because the repair-men charge double on account of the parking tickets they get as soon as they arrive. Mayfair people don't cook, because they haven't paid the gas bill. They order in. Sometimes they invite friends round and hope they will order in for them. On a good day they take the fish fingers out of the deep freeze.

Mayfair people have nannies rather than au pairs and even when they have au pairs they call them nannies. Some Mayfair families have several nannies so that they can look after the grown-ups as well as the children. Mayfair nannies are fiercely loyal because they suspect that Mayfair parents are not suitable parents at all, which is probably true. All the same, Mayfair mothers are very prolific. They are prolific whether or not they have taken their marriage vows. This is so that Mayfair men can never completely abandon them. Their fertility comes as a great shock to everybody in Mayfair. Usually they claim to have been breezing through life on a quarter of an ovary with not a chance in hell of conceiving. When they do conceive anyway it is a matter of some concern to Mayfair men. It is of even more concern when it happens again. And again. Mayfair men usually have at least four small mouths to feed—not to mention the four others they may be feeding somewhere else in the world, for Mayfair husbands are just as devious as Mayfair wives and usually have several families scattered around the globe without anyone suspecting anything at all. They are able to do this because they are globe-trotters. The Mayfair husband scarcely stays in one place for as much as a weekend at a time. Often his wife has no idea where he is. He will call her from Hamburg or Cape Town or Caracas or Amman explaining how he has been held up on business. Mayfair husbands never intend to go away for long which is why they never leave enough housekeeping and why Mayfair nannies get so hungry that they take their employers to McDonald's and treat them out of their own savings.

All the same, Mayfair children are always well turned out. They all wear designer clothes and are extremely catty about people who do not shop in Saks Fifth Avenue. They all go to private schools in Kensington, they take gym lessons in Knightsbridge and swimming lessons in Holland Park and skiing lessons in Alperton, and piano lessons at home and ballet lessons at Mme Vacani or Miss Ballantine—and all this with no visible means of support. No matter that Mayfair used to have one of the best state primary schools in the world, Mayfair mothers insist on sending their offspring to school out of the area. It makes no difference to them. Mayfair mothers never get up in the early mornings and take the children themselves. They never bother much about their school reports. What you learn in Mayfair is not as important as who you know. Mayfair mothers always ask their children's teachers back for gins and tonics and give them birthday presents. Consequently Mayfair children do very well at school.

Mayfair people are always secretive about how they earn their money, particularly if they are currently doing well. Whereas Hampstead people tell other people what they are doing all of the time and Chelsea people tell other people what they are doing even when they are not doing it, Mayfair people never tell anybody anything at all. Mayfair wives never even ask their husbands what they do. They never ask questions so they never have to answer them in return. Besides they do not *want* to know the answers. They might be forced to take a moral stand. Mayfair men describe themselves as entrepreneurs. Other people describe themselves as something in insurance or something in import-export, or something in property or some sort of advisor to the government. This usually means something to do with international arms dealing.

Meanwhile their wives do nothing at all. Or certainly that is their story, even if they are running a wildly successful cash business on the side. Mayfair trust is inspired by mutual distrust. No Mayfair wife would ever be seen to be self-supporting in case she suddenly found that that was what she was expected to be. No Mayfair man would ever tell her the extent of his empire in case the day dawned when she used this against him. Mayfair people are always aware of the rainy day around the corner, and they live as if it were going to be tomorrow.

It is almost impossible to get a Mayfair person on the telephone because the line is always busy. Mayfair people telephone a lot. They gossip on the telephone, but they do not gossip for fun like Chelsea people, they gossip for information. It is not wise to tell a Mayfair person anything at all because he will probably make more money out of it than you do. It may be the last piece missing from his jigsaw and get him out of an awful jam, but he will never thank you for it. Mayfair people do not mind what relationships they exploit in order to survive. They have been known to sell their babies for pounds of cocaine, or flaunt their bodies, or publish 'true-life' memoirs. Meanwhile they will tell any lies in order to preserve their respectability.

Mayfair ladies *never* admit to having a sex life, even if

some people think this is what Mayfair is all about.
Mayfair hookers are always *engaged* to *clever, handsome*
men who just *happen* to be rich international diamond
dealers. They are always *heartbroken* that their *fiancés'*
wives refuse to give them a divorce. They are deeply
religious and it is against all their *principles* to live in sin.
They are always invaluable to their fiancés on a *business*
level. They are covered in furs out of *respect* and only stay
in bed late because they have been having a reunion with
their *fathers* the night before. It is due to their *fathers* that
they are *lucky* enough to own their own *little* flats. They
get up at midday to lunch with a *girlfriend*. They keep their
figures in such good trim by playing tennis, and this year
they are lucky enough to have been invited to Marbella, to
stay with *family friends*. It will make such a change from
Las Vegas where they have been doing a little *business*.
Ask them what business and they say, 'The usual.'

Mayfair people never go on holiday. They always travel
on business and they do business in the most convenient
places. They do business in St Moritz at Christmas, in the
Caribbean in the New Year and in Nice in the summer.
Unlike Belgravia people, who like to mix a little business
with pleasure, there is no pleasure in these things at all for
Mayfair people. They are not there for their health. They
simply hate idling around in the sun and they won't sit
still in case they are missing something. They don't play
games to pass the time, they only play games to win.
Mayfair people are competitive and hyperactive. Unlike
Chelsea people (who think exercise spoils their image) and
Hampstead people (who only ever exercise their minds)
Mayfair people are always on the run. They duck and they
dive and they jog and they roller-skate and they fish and
they swim. They are always hopping from pillar to post
and they are always in a hurry even when they have
nowhere to go. They always look marvellous in the midst

of all this activity. They have designer clothes to exercise in and they are never out of breath and they never, ever sweat. They have exercise cycles in their homes and are always having their thighs developed or their livers detoxified.

Mayfair people are very fond of their health. They take ginseng and vitamins A to E and B12 shots and virility pills and pills to keep them awake and pills to send them to sleep. They know more about their own bodies than their doctors do and they know more than any psychiatrist about their minds. They are very superstitious. They have their bumps read and their palms read, and their faces and their fortunes and their charts. Mayfair people will take a chance on anything in the hope of learning some good news. They are scarcely prejudiced at all except in favour of Mayfair. You can spot them immediately when they leave the district because they have a nervous breakdown on the other side of Hyde Park Corner and develop hives going south of the river and north of the park.

5

Belgravia

UNLIKE MAYFAIR PEOPLE, who only know how to borrow money, Belgravia people really do have it although they say they don't.

This is because it is *Tied Up*. Belgravia people own the land we walk on and the property on it, they own the eggs we eat, the bacon, the bread and the pheasants and salmon as well. Not content with this, they own the coal under the land and the oil and the tin and lots of less savoury commodities too. They own porno shops and rock bands and scandal sheets and gambling dens. They own anything or anybody who will show a return on their investment. Belgravia people are born investors, but they rarely learn to be spenders. Sometimes they have millions tied up making more millions but never a ready in sight. They will sit in candlelight beneath the Reynolds and the Landseers studying the share prices and sipping instant coffee, worrying about the day the North Sea will dry up. Meanwhile they may discreetly spoil themselves but they rarely spoil their guests, even if these have come round to give them a hot tip for the 4.30 or to ride them in on a deal in Hong Kong or South America in return for being able to use their names and titles. Belgravia people keep magnums of Cristal in the fridge and jam-jars full of Beluga

caviar, but they offer you cheap sparkling wine and
lumpfish roe. They make Bloody Maries which are very
nearly virginal and top up their own with Stolichnaya
when you disappear to the loo. They lock up the port and
the cellar and turn the central heating off when they lock
the front door. The loo is never heated even when they are
at home. They pour tap water into Malvern bottles for
their house guests and reseal the Perrier after opening it.
When you come to visit, flat Perrier is what you get, or
vapid tonic water and stagnant ginger ale. They gee it up
with a silver swizzle stick and have beautiful manners to
cover up all sorts of deceptions.

While Mayfair people always put on a good show in
order to get a loan, Belgravia people always look im-
poverished so no one asks them for one. Belgravia people
have the true meanness of the very, very rich indeed.
Belgravia people have elevated meanness to the level of an
art. They are never generous to others but this does not
stop them expecting generosity. They are very acquisitive
and better than a good buy they like an exquisite gift. Or
an indefinite loan. Belgravia people cannot be guaranteed
to return anything of value once they have become
accustomed to it. They have long-term plans and short
memories.

Belgravia houses are exquisite. They have the biggest
weeping figs, the newest magazines, the most sparkling
crystal, silver and mahogany. They have the thickest
carpets, the most exquisite paint jobs and the most
sophisticated hangings. They have the furthest flung
souvenirs and the oldest antiques. They have the most
valuable heirlooms and the most modern gadgets. The
houses are a tribute to their lives. Belgravia people are
collectors of things, not people. They know that people do
not last but that acquisitions do—if only you can hold on to
them. They have genuine pictures, curious first editions,

exquisite cars and rambling country houses, but their
town property always looks unlived in, like a museum.
There are net curtains on the windows and velvet drapes
drawn shut and grilles connected to burglar alarms. This is
because this property *is* unlived in. While all this fine
white stucco is accruing in value in Belgravia, its owners
are pounding the moors with hipflasks of elderberry wine
in their Norfolk jackets, hunting foxes in the shires or
leaving their footprints on the beaches of Mustique.
Belgravia people have houses in Berkshire, Hampshire
and Staffordshire, in Scotland, France and the Bermudas.
They are always in the right place at the right time, and if
they are not they leave it immediately and go elsewhere.

Not only are the houses unlived in, the streets are
unlived in too. No matter what day it is, Belgravia streets
are deserted except for Belgravia retainers in grey gabar-
dine raincoats and peaked caps polishing the hubcaps of
Belgravia Rolls Royces. Behind closed doors other Belgravia retainers are ironing the newspapers and the
pound notes and polishing the 50p pieces with Silvo. No
matter how it has been acquired, the pound in the
Belgravia pocket is always pristine.

Unlike Mayfair business, which is done at 'meetings',
Belgravia business is done in bed or round the dinner table
or aboard the yacht or the new Mystère executive jet.
Unlike Chelsea people, who simply go away for the
pleasures of the flesh, Belgravia people always like to
combine business with pleasure. They never go to the
beach without a backgammon board, or to a new island
without wanting to develop it. Belgravia people always
have yachts and executive jets to facilitate these pursuits
because they know they might as well spend their profits
on such essential testimonials to their enduring personal
worth as pay taxes to some parvenu government to fritter
away on the social services or the armed forces. Such

personal modes of transport enable Belgravia people to shore up their funds offshore without any paperwork so that these manoeuvres can be kept totally secret from their retainers and from their wives. They employ versatile Jewish, English-based accountants to make sense of their apparent insular poverty. And they run up huge debts at Harrods, the butcher, the wine merchant and the tailor. They never owe their bookmaker, marry their mistresses or pay full price for any other used goods. Belgravia people shop at all the right places, though they rarely pay the asking price. Dressmakers and bootmakers, shirt-makers and hairdressers, purveyors of poultry and lamb cutlets, of linen and china, are only too glad to let them have their wares at discount because they are so well connected. Belgravia people borrow their frocks on approval and return them with regret slightly soiled the next day. Suppliers to Belgravia people never press for truth on these occasions lest they be seen to be undermining the fabric of Empire whereby they also live. In hard times Belgravia people do not tighten their belts, they invest even more money. Hard times are good times to invest. If times are really hard they disappear. Lord Lucan lived in Belgravia.

They invest in Mercedes and Ferraris and Corniches and black Minis with chrome overriders and fog lights and smoked windows and telephones to use when they get stuck in boring traffic jams. They speak· on them even when they are not stuck. The man who nearly flies into you around Hyde Park Corner because he is holding an animated conversation with his New York stockbroker and making notes at the same time is either on his way to or from his home in Belgravia. Belgravia people have a lot of telephones, and they have banks of televisions so they can watch four channels, Prestel and Ceefax at the same time. They have amplified telephones and scrambled telephones, but if they hold amplified conversations they do so to some very good purpose for Belgravia people are very self-conscious, and they can be very discreet. Unlike people in Hampstead and Chelsea they always hold their personal conversations in private. They are much more discreet than Mayfair people. Belgravia people are so discreet they do not even share bedrooms with their husbands or wives.

Belgravia people marry for prestige as well as money, and certainly never for love. Belgravia people have Arrangements. Since they invariably have several properties, they divide them amongst themselves to their mutual advantage. It is not uncommon for Belgravia couples to spend no time together at all, but they do not think of their marriages as unhappy. On the contrary, Belgravia people have some of the happiest marriages in the country precisely because they only see each other at special occasions: conceptions, births, marriages and deaths. These are the times when they come into their fortunes, leaving them free the rest of the time to play with much less privileged people who are more fun and are only too glad of the action which they would not get otherwise. Even when Belgravia couples do live under the same roof, they are accustomed to having nights off. This is described as doing business or protecting their interests. It is extremely sophisticated and can only be mastered with generations of practice. Non-practitioners who accidentally marry into Belgravia through some temporary mutual aberration, rarely if ever last the course. Sometimes even Belgravia people would rather not last it but this is regarded as lily-livered, lower-class and astigmatic. On the whole, Belgravia marriages are enduring, even if they are enduring hell. Belgravia love-affairs are with figures who are not their spouses. These figures are usually to be found in a ledger.

Training for this kind of life takes precedence over potty training if you live in Belgravia. Belgravia people do not only train their children to knock on bedroom doors before they enter, they also train their spouses. On the other hand, Belgravia staff are allowed to come and go at will. It is they who know all about the habits of their employers and act as their sounding boards, their nursemaids, their procurers and their apologists. Some Belgravia employees share the habits of their employers, and this is all right by Belgravia people as long as the servants know their place and stick to it. There is rarely any choice in the matter. Belgravia people keep their servants, their tradesmen and even their children on a pittance. They tie up the children's inheritance in the hands of decrepit Dickensian trustees and wonder why their sons fall in love with rich divorcées. Belgravia people do not like their children because they are younger than they are and all set to have a better time. Belgravia parents want to make absolutely sure the family is not undermined by any eccentricity within it except their own. This means Belgravia is a hotbed of eccentricity as generations vie with each other to get control of the stakes. Within those noble whitewashed portals many a blood feud is shaping up nicely.

Belgravia people put their children in the care of other people as soon as possible. In early life this means below stairs on the country estate where they freeze to death with the dogs and the servants. At the age of seven they are sent away to boarding school while Mama and Papa are having a good time in Town. In due course, they go to Eton or Harrow, Mama is packed off to the country house and Papa is left having a good time in Town. Mama spends her time gros-pointing the ancestral fire-screens. Because they seldom see them, Belgravia people have terra cotta drawings done of their children, their wives and their dogs by fashionably mediocre artists and are more familiar with the pictures than they are with the real thing. They also have romantic photographs taken at great expense by titled photographers to stand on the grand piano which nobody plays. This is the only use for the grand piano.

Belgravia children who do not complete their education learning ferocious traditional English rituals in ferocious traditional English public schools go to Switzerland to be finished off. Switzerland is full of Belgravia children whose parents pay as much as £25,000 a year each to have them learn how to ski. They learn to schuss and to slalom, to sunbathe and to smoke. They also learn a lot of good telephone numbers and how to get the best table in the best restaurant in Rome, Paris and New York. That is about all they learn. Belgravia children are ignorant in three languages and never fluent in their own. Sometimes they affect strange little accents having never heard English spoken during their formative years. If they do not learn how to speak they certainly do not learn how to write. In the words of one Swiss finishing school master: 'Why should I teach you? All you need to write once you leave here is your signature at the bottom of a cheque.'

Belgravia people have absolutely no interest in culture except as an investment. They are far too interested in real life to ever get a vicarious kick out of the stage or the concert hall unless it be to proposition someone on it. They like pictures because pictures are unique objects which will be bought by someone else unless they can get their hands on them first. They never sell their houses because they know that Belgravia property only comes on the market once in a lifetime and if they lose it it will never come their way again. Belgravia people like jewellery only when it is the real thing. For them the real thing is Belgravia, and outsiders begin at Knightsbridge. They hate usurpers, interlopers, spies, suckers and anybody with any imagination. Belgravia people have no imagination of their own whatsoever and whatever the Royal Family does is good enough for them. After all the back garden of Buck House backs on to Belgravia.

Belgravia people never go to church except to weddings, births and funerals, but they agree with everything it stands for except immortality. They never divorce if they can help it so that they never have to divide up the spoils. Belgravia divorces, when they happen, are especially bitter and ex-wives are kept in direst poverty in the far reaches of Fulham. When ex-children come to visit the servants are sent on sabbatical to give the impression there aren't any, and the Rolls is kept parked out of sight a mile away.

Belgravia people never have rows with their children except through a third party. In the beginning it is nanny; from then on it is the family solicitor. Consequently Belgravia children are much closer to nanny and the family solicitor than they ever are to their parents. This accounts for their flamboyant behaviour with which they hope to attract the attention of one or other parent sooner or later. These gestures are always useless because Belgravia parents are lost in their own flamboyant gestures and are trying to attract the attention of someone else. Belgravia people know from an early age that their parents are the most selfish people they know, which accounts for a good deal of cynicism about the world. Their selfishness goes on well into old age. Belgravia people try and keep going for ever in the hope that eventually they will outlive all the rest of the opposition and come into the entire family inheritance. They try and promote extreme longevity with the aid of expensive doctors in Mexico, Switzerland and the Philippines, some of whome are quite as cynical as themselves and often a good deal more phoney. They pay thousands of pounds and dollars and francs, yen, guilder, marks and dhiram for face-cream, face-lifts, organ transplants and remedies against gout, and have sheeps' placentæ injected into their human bodies against the ravages of time and human fantasy. They will try absolutely anything to stop their children getting their hands on the money they consider their own. Naturally it never works: Belgravia people are buried with much ceremony and little sympathy and they are never, ever mourned at all.

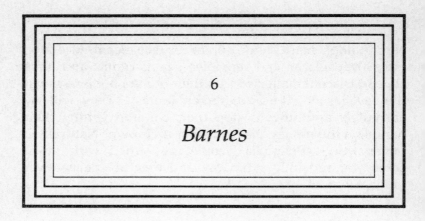

6

Barnes

ONCE THERE WAS a classic movie called *Bend of the River*. It starred Jimmy Stewart and Rock Hudson and Stepin Fetchit and it was full of fire and adventure and pioneer spirit. Barnes lies tucked into one of the biggest bends in any river, but this film was not made in Barnes. There is not a lot of fire and adventure and pioneer spirit in Barnes people. There are not many Stepin Fetchits to do for them. There are, however, a lot of television actors with real old treasures and au pairs who do instead.

Barnes is conveniently close to the BBC television studios as the crow flies. It is also on the roads to Twickenham, Shepperton, Ealing and Pinewood, where sometimes even now you may still catch a glimpse of a gaffer or a grip or a best boy. Barnes is known as Hollywood-on-Thames. Camera-men, make-up artists, continuity girls who live in Barnes can reckon to be on the set in the film studios within half an hour of leaving their front door. BBC producers, comedy stars and series writers who try to get to Wood Lane in half an hour can only do it by helicopter. It almost always takes longer to get to the TV Centre than to get to Bucks, Bray or Teddington. It takes almost as long to get to Lime Grove as to get to Elstree. This is because of Hammersmith Bridge.

Hammersmith Bridge is a very handsome bridge for those who enjoy looking at bridges. It is an iron bridge and one of the most handsome bridges in the country. Sometimes it is painted sky blue, sometimes mustard yellow. Hammersmith Bridge seems to get a new paint job more regularly than the Forth Bridge, and every time it gets a new paint job it is closed to traffic. On the rare occasions it is open it is a very narrow bridge. It is also a very short bridge. It is the shortest route into Barnes from London proper. For those who have to cross it rather than look at it, it is, therefore, a very annoying bridge indeed. There is nothing more annoying than realising what a brief distance separates you from your destination and knowing that there is nothing whatsoever you can do about it. There are many people who live in Barnes who have taken the decision never to try and cross it. Once across, many Barnes people limit their sights accordingly.

When Barnes people talk about going up to town they mean making the effort to get to Hammersmith. When Barnes people talk of going *into* town they mean going to the local shopping parade. Metropolitan life has very little to do with Barnes. In Putney, separated by nothing more than an invisible Domesday line across the verdant amalgam of Barnes and Putney Commons, the breath of the big city can be felt down the neck of the most bourgeois inhabitant. Putney people are brusque, brisk and urban. Putney people want to get on with it. Putney people snap at you in the shops and hate to pass the time of day. Barnes people muddle along as if the twentieth century had never dawned. Shopping in Barnes is an event rather than a chore. There is always time to chat over the change no matter how long the queue is. There is always time to gossip over someone's varicose veins, to chuck someone's child under the chin and admire his astonishing growth rate, to verbally redecorate the living

room with your nextdoor neighbour or to occupy the
telephone box with long calls to your sister-in-law about
pastry-making. There is always time for speculation with
the gasman, a cup of tea with the milkman, or a discussion
about hooliganism, town-planning, pruning, package
tours, bottling, the Boat Race and what the Government
should do about nursery schools with the local green-
grocer. A great many exciting exchanges happen in Barnes
shops. A great deal of information is swapped, and
lascivious glances, and a great deal of snooping goes on
into other people's shopping baskets.

People in Barnes invariably do their own shopping no
matter how familiar their faces. This is no doubt because
of the absence of Stepin Fetchits. It is also because it is
something to do. Barnes is full of faces you almost
recognise if only you could put a name to them. You can
tell that they are in show business because their shopping
baskets are full of fish fingers and TV dinners, rather than
roast beef. This is not so much because they are out of
work and cannot afford the roast beef, but because they
plan to save time cooking by living off TV dinners so they
can spend more of the day watching themselves on TV
while they eat them. They go round to each other's houses
and spend time looking at each other on TV. When they
cannot get near a TV set themselves they make sure they
have a video machine to record themselves on TV so they
can watch themselves later. When they are not watching
themselves they go for a drink at the Sun and spend the
time discussing their performances.

The Sun is one of those mysterious gathering places
which people visit from all over London for some reason
committed to tribal memory, even though it has the same
hunting horns, the same beermats and the same tankards
hanging from the beams as any other tarted-up pub. On
Saturday and Sunday lunchtimes the Sun is full of people

in cable-knit sweaters who voted for Mrs Thatcher, slapping each other on the back and looking for a little reported action safely out of the immediate range of any personal danger. You can tell which ones are the actors because they are keeping a restless eye on two doors at once, trying to see who is about to make an entrance. As often as not it will not be another actor at all, but some ambitious chick who has specially braved the crossing of the whole of London and Hammersmith Bridge expressly to meet a TV actor. Chicks in Barnes do not wear purple hairdos and punk clothes like chicks in Notting Hill or Chelsea; neither do they wear flatties and parkas like the majority of Barnes mums. Barnes chicks teeter along in stiletto boots, in skintight jeans and cinctured raincoats which might have been borrowed from Humphrey Bogart and which is the sort of uniform which appeals to Barnes actors. Barnes chicks can tell an actor before he gets out of his obligatory BMW by the way he will always do five minutes' business for any kid hanging around the carpark. At home he practises in front of the refrigerator on his own kids.

There are a great many kids in Barnes and on the whole they have a much better time of it than Barnes mums. They have more expensive haircuts, prettier clothes and a better education, which is to say private. They have more treats, more meals out and even when they are wandering around the streets they get to feed the ducks on the pond and score a takeaway hamburger. Education, though expensive, is not actually pertinent to the Barnes way of life, though the expense is. If Barnes children fail to do well at one school they are simply manipulated into another similar school which has more reason to be glad of the fees. Social improvement is paramount. Barnes children are much improved socially by a Shirley Temple bow in the hair, individually imported American clothes (which are a testimonial to their father's travels), and their cute convivial tricks which can range from anything from a ballet solo to a turn on the catwalk. Entertainment is a structural part of their existence. When there is no professional entertainment available they go to the Barnes Fair. Barnes mums get to organise the Barnes Fair.

Barnes mums love organising. They are always getting together and forming playgroups and summer schools and holding second-hand clothing sales and garage sales and car-boot sales and complaining how busy they are and finding time to write about it in the community newsletter. Barnes people love to get together and the Community Centre is the focal point of their local desires. They are always encouraging each other to learn local history on a Monday, to do slimming classes on a Tuesday and to take elementary Spanish on a Wednesday so they can communicate with the new au pair. On the whole there is always a new au pair. Au pairs are very short lived in Barnes, partly because of the social ambitions of Barnes mums which are rarely fulfilled (which failure is blamed on the slovenliness of the help); and partly because the help cannot get across Hammersmith Bridge quick enough and up to Piccadilly Circus, which was the whole reason to come here anyway. Barnes mothers have a bottomless supply of au pairs. They need to get away on a Thursday for landscape painting or pottery, on a Friday for the drama group and to join the brass band on Saturday. On Sunday morning they form posses to clean up the common, on Sunday afternoon they attend a symposium in someone's front room on the latest trend in French cinema. No one in Barnes knows much about these things, but they are jolly busy doing them. Barnes mothers have no time to write full-length books about them like Hampstead mothers. They still have to fit in one afternoon with the old age pensioners, an hour a week for handmade jewellery classes, another for handpainted textiles and appliquéd cushions. Barnes shops are often persuaded to market their efforts at flexible prices. Barnes handicrafts may look interesting but they may not be a solid investment. The clasps may snap or the hems may fray, and, as Princess Grace found when she bought a hand-tinted dinner set from an amateur, if you put such a thing in your dishwasher it may come out blank from the detergent.

Barnes mothers invariably have dishwashers and they have no guilt about using them as do Hampstead mothers. They are obsessed with cleaning. After they have organ-ised their children and other people's children, and the school run and their husbands—who don't take much organising because they are normally out of the country—and the new church and next Sunday lunch and their dogs and their nextdoor neighbours and their out-of-town families, they turn around and wash the kitchen curtains. All this leaves them with very little time to spend on their actual selves. This is a cautionary tale, because Barnes mothers used to be very keen indeed on themselves. They were the ones who used to be found in the stiletto boots, skintight jeans and cinctured raincoats with which they snared Barnes men in the first place. All the provocative chicks who round up child-loving actors in the carpark of the Sun or elsewhere become mumsy in Barnes in no time at all. They sit round discussing how mumsy they are while all the actors sit round the TV, the writers lock themselves in their studios and all the other men, who are roadies and agents, are either still in the pub or up town, secure in the knowledge that they have done the right thing by their wives by sticking them in such a desirable suburb as Barnes. People from town are always trying to get invited to Barnes so they can be mumsified by Barnes mothers. Barnes mothers will mumsify anything on legs.

They cannot sit still. They get up in the middle of lunch to make tea and in the middle of dinner to take the dog for a walk.

Barnes dogs are very large, and so is the evidence they leave behind them. The evidence of other people's dogs always infuriates Barnes people. The transgressions of other people's dogs are to Barnes people what non-Hampstead cigarette smokers are to Hampstead non-smokers. They rail on about their foul habits at dinner parties and leave the room in the presence of owners responsible for canine offenders. They are particularly offended when Putney dogs stray across the invisible boundary on the communal common and leave their first editions on the immaculate Barnes side. The evidence is universally ascribed to Putney dogs despite the fact that everyone in either area owns a similarly large breed. They own Dalmatians and wolfhounds and springers and Labradors and retrievers and setters and Alsatians and great Danes and Pyreneans and, failing all else, super-mongrels which Barnes people defiantly walk in their own bird sanctuary by the river—which may be perfect for the dogs but can hardly be so amusing for the birds. The bird sanctuary is indeed by the river, but visitors to Barnes—those who do not use Hammersmith Bridge but favour a foray in from the hinterland—could be forgiven not only for not noticing the bird sanctuary but also for not noticing the river. The Thames at Barnes is almost invisible behind the barricade of various institutions and a concrete wall. People who live in houses on its banks cannot actually see it unless they stand on a chair in the attic. Other people have to peek at it, according to their inclinations, from the Harrods depository, from Colet Court, the jazz room at the Bull's Head or the riverside Swedish school, which is no doubt situated in Barnes to accommodate all the illegitimate children of those notoriously permissive

Swedish au pairs.

It is not just the au pairs who are accommodating in Barnes. Barnes people put themselves out to be accommodating. They are helpful and neighbourly and always in and out of other people's houses and always enjoying it. Barnes people are charming, Barnes houses are charming, Barnes itself is verdant and village-like. There are no burglars and even if there are, Barnes people are insulted by burglar alarms. It is all undeniably nice. People who live in SW13 count themselves very lucky. People who don't are apt to find that, as with the river, all this sweetness drives them completely round the bend.

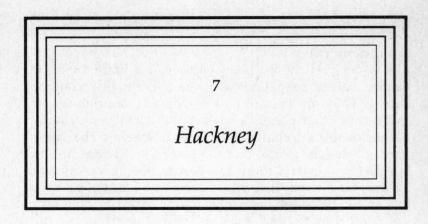

7

Hackney

NOT SO LONG ago they delivered the last giant strawberry cream gâteau to a Well Street bakery in Hackney. Hackney is once again going through a process of change. Tenants of the weather-stained council high-rises and run-down private slums look forward to change, though not necessarily to the dearth of strawberry cream gâteaux. It's just that at five pounds each nobody can afford to buy them. At thirty per cent nobody can afford the rent increases.

There is a lot of change needed in Hackney. It would be nice to see a coat of paint on some of the boarded-up old houses. It would be nice to see the fine old terraces reclaimed and some improvement in the quality of post-war architecture. There is some very fine pre-war architecture, which may come as a surprise to people who live there who are accustomed to seeing it destroyed virtually beyond recognition by the passage of time, and to people who do not who are accustomed to thinking of Hackney as some ad hoc East End bomb-site even before the bombs came. It may come as a surprise to them also to know that John Strype, who used to cast his antiquarian eye on the city in the manner of Boswell, described Hackney as a 'pleasant, healthful town where divers nobles had their seats'. It had many magnificent institutional landmarks, was and is a stronghold of charitable foundations, of dissenting religious sects and unprejudiced community spirit perpetuated today in its campaigning local newspapers.

It was indeed the Sunningdale of former times, full of boarding schools for young ladies of impeccable breeding stock who used to be written about in the old *Tatler*. It was the market garden of London and supplied the horticultural advisor to Catherine the Great. It inspired writers like Daniel Defoe, whose young son, also Daniel, is buried in a Hackney churchyard. It was rich enough to inspire visitors like Dick Turpin who was a frequent guest at various Hackney inns even when he was not actually invited. Hackney has fifteen hundred years of recorded history, which is more than can be said for the gilded ghettoes of today: Belgravia, St John's Wood, or even Westminster. Not that there is no money left in Hackney at all, or that it is invisible. Brash and brand new Jaguars and Mercedes prowl round in places while the rest of Hackney limps along on foot, on bicycle or in fenderless old Vauxhalls. There is money, but it is not perfectly distributed. This is not entirely a bad thing. Hackney is changing in one way today because the property is so reasonably priced compared with its up-and-come neighbour Islington that the professional young middle classes can afford to buy into its Edwardian terraces, thus bolstering its faltering economy and offering once more the possibility of a market in giant strawberry cream gâteaux. Edwardian terraces in Hackney resemble nothing so much as the Edwardian terraces of fashionable Clapham with the added interest that they are nearer the City, which is where many of the young professional middle classes work.

You can immediately spot the newcomers' houses. They are the ones who have done away with the turquoise striped curtains and hung up the rattan blinds instead.

They have removed the fringed lampshades and put up Habitat fixtures. They have ripped out the neon-patterned carpet and polished up the wooden floorboards. They have painted the orange geometric wallpaper white. They have moved out the lime green Dralon armchairs and put in the bent cane. They have replaced the black Nagahide sofa with a pine framed double convertible bed and the tin bath with a stainless steel sink. They have put poinsettias in the place of the aspidistras and paved the garden where the rubbish tip once was. They have left enough room to walk round the tables and chairs rather than trip over them. Old style Hackney residents watch these improvements with curiosity. 'When they have done up the house,' they say to each other, 'they will order in the furniture.' They confidently expect to see from behind their net curtains a furniture van disgorging a lot of furry lilac poufs, plastic chandeliers, maroon and gilded china knick-knacks which will be put on the window ledges facing out to the street. When they see the cream paint appearing on the front doors they tell each other it is an undercoat which will eventually end up the regulation savage purple, hot pink or chrome yellow like all the other houses in the street.

Old style Hackney residents do not mind the new-comers. Or do they? They themselves would rather move out of Hackney. Or would they? Hackney people are confused. They surmount their inconveniences with a friendliness which has elsewhere gone out of style while feeling like little green aliens in their own backyards. Thirty years ago, when most of them were young, we lived in a very different country. Sometimes it is so different that it doesn't seem to be England at all but some place which, with its clean typefaces and concrete cultural centres, might be a part of post-hostility Germany, or with its uniform TV, pop, jogging and roller-skating is an

Americanised holiday camp. A motorised country where nobody gossips on the street corners any more in pinnies and carpet slippers and duster kerchiefs. Where nobody discusses street politics over the washing line or dares throw a bucket of water over the neighbour's tom cat. Where nobody speaks to each other in the shops, where, on the contrary, people are silent and ill-mannered at the check-outs, mesmerised by brandnames, confused by decimalisation, overwhelmed by the need to conform to a style which is so tastefully reticent it almost does not exist. Where everyone knows their rights but no one quite knows how to assert them.

Hackney people do their best. Hackney is neither tasteful nor reticent. There is no jogging in Hackney and you may still smoke on the street. Hackney in its nostalgia is defiant and unashamed. It advertises its habits even when they are not very chic. Hackney shopkeepers pile their wares on the pavements outside their shops. Inside they put everything hopefully on display: they hang dozens of bras next to dozens of scrubbing brushes and lots of lipsticks next to tons of dinky toys. Chain store architecture, the ultimate leveller in the egalitarian society, is a recent arrival. There is no such thing as McDonald's— Hackney people are still grateful for the Wimpy Bar—and there is scarcely a sit-down restaurant in the place. There is one wine bar which is likely to have two customers on a Saturday night—and most of Hackney council on a Friday lunch. There is nowhere to meet but the corner shop or the eel and pie place. The shops still have their traditional façades. Middle-class London only preserves those memories in the form of toy displays sold in over-priced boutiques and made by a handful of dying craftsmen for a generation of children who think that fish come in fingers and oranges grow on the end of frozen lolly sticks. Hackney butchers have their original brass fittings, their murderous meathooks, their green glass signs and striped awnings. They dispense full-bodied cuts complete with atmospheric pollution to families who will only ever grow up to buy their roasts khaki-coloured and cling-film-wrapped from the supermarket deep-freeze.

Hackney is like all our yesterdays. The window displays are half-empty. The panes are faintly grimy. The shops sell mint humbugs and jelly babies from big old screw-top jars. They sell them by the handful in little home-made bags and they sell them singly to children on the way home from school. They sell toffee apples and whelks, lurid icecream and dried-up sausage rolls. They also sell Swiss buns. Bite into a Swiss bun if you have had an adolescence of Swiss buns and you will instantly become a proletarian Proust recalling a whole mundane life-style. A world where a queue is an invitation to a party, a shop is an invitation to queue. Where the baker sells half-loaves of bread, not whole, and his customers wear hand-knit cardigans and carry string bags. Where young and old wheel their laundry round in granny carts and carry their shopping on old prams. Where shops have proud titles like 'Bon Marché', but the goods are not French as the name suggests, nor good, nor particularly good value. It is a world of dripping sandwiches and malt loaves, of kippers and sweet strong tea, of oil-skin tablecloths and gas fires which toast the face and leave the rest of the body freezing. A world where the Swarfega stands next to the HP sauce on the draining board, where dogs are allowed to scavenge and cats still catch mice and the church social is the most fun, and the radio meanwhile is forever tuned to racing results or the football draws, and rumbles on in the background from morning till night. A world of make-shift and of the wink and the nod and the lucky break.

Need something in Hackney? No problem. Someone will know someone whose mother knows someone who knows where to get it at half the displayed price. An MOT for your car? Someone has a friend whose cousin has an uncle who owns a garage. A spare part? The uncle of the cousin of the friend can find it at a moment's notice or whip one up in fibreglass somewhere under the railway arches down past the pub on the left, where he works. A tip on the dogs? Someone has a system which has never failed. A ride into town? No sooner said than done. Half the taxi drivers live in Hackney, which is as it should be considering they are driving Hackney cabs.

The name appears to be an accident of history. A Hackney cab is a cab pulled by a hackney, a hack, an old workhorse. Hackney itself is called for Hacon's Ey—the island of a Dark Age Dane who plundered his way to landowning. Self-improvement, if not plundering, is more dear to Hackney people than Hackney itself. Hackney people have an eye to the main chance and they will push outwards to the benefits of its fringe neighbourhoods if they can. Blacks will move to Stoke Newington, whites along the Ball's Pond Road to Islington or out to Essex, Turks and Greeks to Finsbury Park and thence to Muswell Hill. They may not move entirely without regret. They may not be moved in upon by the young professional middle classes entirely without regret. Watch out, Hackney, for those bewildering, militant, conformist manifestations of affluent leisure which compulsively accompany an apparent break: for jogging and gyms, faggots and feminism, boutiques and hypermarkets and no smoking demands. Watch out for the urge to convert absolutely everyone to the same utterly rational, totally admirable and unutterably wet point of view where everyone may be able to afford a strawberry cream gâteau, but nobody will actually be able to eat it because they are all deeply into slavishly watching their figures.

8

Limehouse

THERE IS AT least one Limehouse resident who would
have the rest of the country believe that his particular neck
of the Thames rivals Runnymede as the riverside scene of
the most momentous event in the history of British
democracy. After the Magna Carta, the Limehouse Declaration: the first announcement of the parturition of a soon-
to-be Centre Party from the ailing body of British Socialism
as represented by Michael Foot, soon-to-be nicknamed
Worzel Gummidge. The Magna Carta was a declaration of
civil liberties presented in 1215 by a rugged nobility to a
licentious king in the open meadows near Royal Windsor.
The Limehouse Declaration was an expression of wishful
thinking delivered in 1981 to a nation raised on free milk
and Disney cartoons from a smart terrace in London's
otherwise depressed East End. Within a year the four
originators of the Social Democratic Party could be heard
squabbling amongst themselves just like everyone else in
the big playpen up the river. The SDP quads had an
aggravated problem of sibling rivalry: they could never
make up their mind which toy they wanted to play with.

Indecision is a problem which attaches to Limehouse
itself: is it radical, is it chic, is it democratic or downright

insulting to start a fashionable colony in down-trodden dockland? Cross the Commercial Road, make your way south towards the river and you will find yourself in a part of east London which has very little in common with the rest of east London. The Limehouse colony hugs a couple of hundred yards of water facing the industrial landscape of Rotherhithe where once great barges loaded and unloaded at working docks and piers. Today it is a little pocket of privilege populated by personalities who are so liberal they are not sure what to believe beyond the one certainty that, geographically at least, they are situated way out on a limb. The limb that is Limehouse lies in the heart of proletarian country with none of the usual proletarian conveniences like, for instance, a good public transport system. This ensures a certain amount of the privacy which is a fashionable affectation of artists, actors, TV presenters and politicians who make their living by clamouring for attention.

Fashionable liberals in New York, London and Paris love to live in depressed areas because of what they call 'Space'. This does not necessarily mean that they get a lot more space than anyone who lives in more conventional areas, but that they pay a lot less for the right to occupy it—if they get it at the right time, that is. If not they get it at twice the price. This can seem quite extravagant if what you actually get is to camp in a dank warehouse with no heating, plumbing or cooking facilities and a brisk wind coming off the estuary. Those who are with us this far then get to spend twice as much again as anyone who lives in a custom-built space because of the price of labour today. By the time they have pointed the brickwork, put in a damp course, staved off the tide and restored the floorboards to the original condition, they are lucky if they have enough left over to pay for the electricity, the telephone and the petrol to get all the way out there—

usually on a moped, this being the essence of liberal chic.

Limehouse is do-it-yourself with bucks. Typical Lime-house conversions are impossible to sell because they are so expensive, unless you sell them to other fashionable liberals who are not, however, prepared to buy them because it is not considered properly avant-garde to inherit someone else's taste. Naturally it is also too expensive. Fashionable people living for the same invest-ment in the heart of Belgravia are apt to dismiss the attraction of the Limehouse way of life. This is only because they are such philistines. New intellectuals love Limehouse just as the new rich love St John's Wood. They love all the difficulties entailed in living there, never mind getting there. There is nowhere to send the children to school, nowhere to shop for the food, furniture, frocks or pictures which flatter walls of other chic liberals. Lime-house liberals therefore make a complicated philosophy out of this state of affairs. Naturally they know all about the virtues of French cooking, Italian sports cars, private education and Persian cats, but to vaunt such perceptions would be an act of mindless, unprincipled and bourgeois materialism. It would also be extremely tactless in the East End where old age pensioners still save to buy four cigarettes out of a pack of twenty and children beg from their prams through no fault of their own. Limehouse liberals patronise the same stores as Limehouse locals with the result that *The Times Literary Supplement* lies side by side with the *Hackney Gazette*. Limehouse liberals do not see daily shopping as an art form, nor children as a necessity in an overcrowded world. They are much keener on cats, which are much better at keeping away the Limehouse rats.

Limehouse liberals are not ascetics. They do not aim to live in isolation, in discomfort on bare boards with nothing but the scenery as scenery. They like possessions of a sort.

They like artefacts and knick-knacks, souvenirs and bric-à-brac, lead soldiers and chrome bumpers, juke boxes, pottery ducks, Shakespeare busts, Staffordshire money boxes and New England quilts. They fill their houses with the sort of junk their mothers threw away the moment they could afford anything better, and wait for the next retrospective to come round at the Hayward to prove just how sensitive they are. Limehouse liberals are nostalgic. Limehouse plumbers, electricians and chars who do for Limehouse liberals are not nostalgic at all. They only do for these people because they have seen them on telly. They know that the good old days were not so good after all and that none of the 'interesting pieces' has any resale value in Limehouse proper. They know that you will not find many ethnic scatter cushions, 'Thirties mantelpieces and broken console radios falling off a barrow in preference to a good working 26-inch colour television set.

Limehouse liberals just love scatter cushions all over their bare floorboards. There is nowhere comfortable to sit, sleep, eat or cook, and no privacy in Limehouse at all because everyone in a converted warehouse must be in a position at all times to appreciate their remarkable view of the river. There is very little actual work done for the same reason. It is much easier to admire the sky, the seagulls and the changing tides outside than to concentrate on any internal self-improvement. This means that Limehouse liberals live permanently with a pervading sense of insufficiency and enjoy prostrating themselves for some greater aesthetic and social cause. Limehouse correspondingly supplies the causes: Limehouse is undoubtedly aesthetic because Turner painted the river there, and there is variegated socialism all around in the shape of countless housing estates.

Limehouse liberals are not always aware of the housing estates. They live in a row of identically shabby (from the

outside) houses to the leeward, identically boarded and
veiled to prevent the intrusion into the liberal retina of a
less imaginative way of life. They are identically scruffy to
discourage any misplaced darts of envy. Limehouse liberals paint their façades in varying abominable shades of
blue according to the precise degree of flamboyance of the
personality of the individual occupant. 'The Limehouse
Blues' no longer refers to a poignant piece of jazz music.
'The Gang of Four' is no longer an oblique tribute to
Limehouse's seedy past as the centre of London's
Chinatown. Do not go looking these days for Fu Manchu
in Limehouse. Chinatown has resettled itself in Soho.
Limehouse Chinese have perfect second generation sec-
ondary modern accents which have not yet invaded
Gerrard Street.

Fifteen years ago, when Jacob Rothschild and Andrew
Sinclair first established an establishment bridgehead on
Narrow Street, there was more establishment Limehouse
life around. You could still smell the coal dust from the
pregnant barges as they rounded Limehouse Reach, you
could still hear the river gnawing away at your expensively shored up foundations, you could still burn the driftwood in your open grate. These days of double-glazing
and artificial coal fires have put an end to all that. Today
you can run the river against your plate-glass window as if
it were a silent movie. You can nip downstairs, not to a
pint of coarse English ale, but a litre of mass-produced
French wine in the new wine bar. It is a far cry in the
Grapes from the days when Alice West exhibited her
picture of Saturday night drinkers in that pub in the Royal
Academy in 1949. Then it was all cloth caps and hessian
overcoats, the dockers imbibing as much smoke with their
beer as in the local opium den. It is an even further cry
from the days of Dickens in this same part of London.
These days nice young men in sheepskin jackets pull

briefly and curiously up in their Jaguars to drink lager and Campari with their girlfriends and a riverside view. The Grapes has been given a facelift which seems to have come straight from the imagination of a master of instant Chelsea nostalgia. There is something theatrical about the facelift they are giving to Limehouse, exiling the river to a piece of scenery that swings in from the flies when it is necessary to the plot.

There was a time when Limehouse people lived from their rough river. Limehouse people would never have been happy up above the tidal waters among the willows and the Criscraft of Oxfordshire and Berks. They were not interested in angling, ducklings and potted ivy. They were one step away from the sea and from ships that had seen the world. The docklands were where the immigrants came in and where they first stayed. Anyone who passed through and caught the tang of the salt and of foreign tongues, felt the tug of adventure which would stay with him forever. From London to Merseyside, to San Francisco, the docks were truly cosmopolitan, not fashionably so, the warehouses were full of functional goods, not recycled kitsch.

The ships have given way to container lorries, that romantic world to potted chic. There should come a day when the docklands with their magnificent shapes and spaces are revived into proper, though different, communities for the people who have known them at their worst. The river is marvellous, and so is its potential, but the present Limehouse community is so artificial that more natural people automatically think twice about dropping anchor there. They are terrified lest some liberal drops in to borrow a cup of sugar and stays all day to discuss the seminal significance of the lesbian single mother over endless cups of scented jasmine tea.

9

London's River

ALMOST EVERYTHING, FROM the English weather to the English public school to the English licensing laws, combines to mark the English as a nation of masochists. And there can be few more masochistic English men, women or children than those who choose voluntarily to live full-time on a houseboat on the tidal Thames. The fact is, however big a boat is, it is always too small. *She* is always too small, as boat people would prefer it. Even a ship is too small, and this is true if she is the largest aircraft-carrier, the biggest oil-tanker or the most luxurious liner. The largest cabin is too cramped, the longest passenger list too short and the shortest cruise too long. Boats are prisons, as Dr Johnson said (though he actually said ships—he didn't mind taking a rowing boat out on the river after a long lunch as long as someone else was doing the rowing). Better a prison than a ship, in his opinion, because a ship is a prison with the added fear of drowning.

Try telling all that to boat people. They won't hear a word said against boats. Boat people are very stoical, very loyal and very earnest. They are also very trapped though they talk inscrutably at great length about freedom. A life on the ocean wave, they trill along with the song, invoking enviable visions of balmy days on the briny where the air is full of flying fish, the hold is full of rum, the loudest sound is the scurrying of the ship's cat and every wreck holds pirates' gold. We joined the navy to see the world, goes the other song, and what did we see? We saw the sea.

Boat people will have none of that. They talk about freedom even if their boat is moored for ever in the shade of Battersea Bridge and their only freedom is to go up and down with the tide every six hours. They talk about freedom even when they may not empty their bathwater on the rising tide, or flush their loo, or leave their ropes uncoiled. Their idea of freedom is the freedom to live within their own rules. The more improbable the enterprise and the smaller the space that it occupies, the more rules there have to be to keep it all ship-shape.

People who cross the oceans in a dinghy, beginning with Christopher Columbus in something not very much bigger, have always known there must be a place for everything. Your hammock must be stowed before you unstow your grog. Real sailors relish all the rules of life below decks. They love hiding their rations away in lockers and unscrewing their furniture from the floor every time they want to rearrange it. They love swabbing down the galley and sluicing out the heads and scrubbing down the decks and hauling in the nets and furling up the flag before battening down the hatch, shinning down the foc's'le and swigging down a tot. Proper seafarers love the ocean choppy or calm. They glide on the ripples and toss on the rollers, they welcome the currents and respect the undertow, they ride the tides and go with the ebb and flow, they run before the wind and weather out the storm, they mind the wash and they sweat out the swell, and white horses would not drag them into any port in a squall. They steer by the stars and fish from the poop.

They bear with the brackish water within and the salt without, with the tang in the breeze and the teeth of the gale, and they scarcely ever fall off the rigging into the drink or bang their heads on the companionway.

Chelsea boatmen always bang their heads on the companionway and they frequently fall off the gangplank. They never bother to stow their waders or hide their cocktail biscuits from the weevils. Chelsea boats are not very spick and span and their masters hardly know a sea-shanty between them. They idly watch the weevils while they float on a slipstream of seltzer and white wine and talk on the telephone to all their landlogged friends just on the other side of the Embankment. Chelsea boat people much prefer being permanently moored to afloat on the waves. They are extremely suspicious of any seaworthy vessel that ties up at their landing stage with tales of derring-do beyond the estuary. Seaworthy vessels rock the boat, so to speak. They set the Thames in unfamiliar motion with their wash, filling up the rotting Chelsea bilges and bursting over their crumbling bulwarks. Chelsea boat people insist on rotting bilges and crumbling bulwarks and there is a pecking order aboard these all-but beached craft based entirely on the present degree of unsuitability for human habitation. Thus a rotten vessel rates full marks while the shippest shapest approaches zero. The perfect houseboat is the one which has every chance of breaking her mooring on a flood tide and sinking without trace before she gets as far as the South Bank. This is known as the romance of boats. A boat with more history than future is inevitably a romantic boat.

Boat people talk about the infinite possibilities of boats, knowing full well that the likelihood is that she will list helplessly into the Thames mud never to rise again after the next low tide. Other people define this as the finite probability of boats. Other finite probabilities are that you will be permanently cold and uncomfortable due to the lack of insulation even if you are not actually drowning, and that you will be driven to desperation by the prosaic intimacies you will be forced to share at the closest of quarters with everyone else on the boat. Or you pick a row with the captain and there is nothing for it but to leave the cabin and shiver your timbers aloft on deck. (Boat people always call each other 'captain' and 'crew' and their neighbours by the name of their boat, be it *Argonaut* or *Discovery*. This is like calling the people at number 25 'Greengables' and the folks at 53 'Fairoaks'.)

Boat owners who try to avoid boat intimacies by embarking on clever conversions are not much admired by their neighbours. They may pile storey after storey on top of some steel hull, coat it with clapboard and call it a boat, but it actually looks like the Cheyne Walk branch of Habitat. It is extraordinary what lengths some landlubbers will go to to disguise an old landing craft in order to have a Cheyne Walk address. Apart from the clapboard they will cover it with Kosset carpet and surround it with duck-board and fill it with directors' chairs and Bonsack baths and Conran lighting and Harrods poufs. They will insulate it with padded walls and double glazing and Venetian blinds. But the plain fact is, once a boat always a boat. They cannot stop the barnacles eroding her bottom and the elements seeping into her superstructure. If you live on a houseboat in Cheyne Walk you may pay up to sixty thousand pounds for these dubious privileges. You may pay a lot less, but you will keep on paying as long as the river keeps washing round your bows and the rain keeps washing down your deck.

Boat people are always adamant about their poverty, but their cash clearly flows quite as well as the Thames. You cannot get a mortgage on a boat because, frankly, it is not likely to pass a survey long enough to get as far as the down payment. Investment is not the point of boat owning, but a certain voyeuristic attitude is. This comes of neither living quite on shore nor on the sea. Neither living quite in the present nor the past. Neither living quite in a house or a caravan or a craft. Neither living quite in dry dock or afloat. Yet even if the boats no longer go anywhere it is important to think they once might have done: that they landed on the beaches of Dunkirk, for example, or earned their living carrying coal. Other boats, in the South of France perhaps, may have gleaming decks, fresh-water showers, central heating and galleys big enough for six *sous-chefs*. The *Christina* may have been built entirely for pleasure, the *Britannia* to fly the flag, but Chelsea boats must in no way be pleasurable, practical or purpose-built. If you need a bath you must take it in the sink. If you need a fire you must first collect the driftwood—and if a shore-party is to be manned, first fish the car-keys out of the knee-high mud.

Boat people enjoy all these hazards. They promote mutual reliability and familiarity. They do not in the least mind spending their days creosoting the decks or empty-ing the chemical toilet, bailing out the bunks or painting the Plimsoll line. They do not even mind spending their nights doing these things. None of this matters to boat people, who, like bedsitter people, have a certain bravado which enjoys surmounting difficulties like trying to cook a six-course meal on a single gas ring, and even believes itself deserving of such difficulties.

Where two or three boat people are gathered together you may confidently expect to find one divorcée, prefer-ably with several children who do not know how to swim, one out-of-work gay and one elderly spinster with a consuming passion which it would be uphill for someone half her age to fulfil. She will be giving piano lessons despite the difficulties of keeping the instrument in tune in the permanent damp. Or she will be trying to win the prize for the best garden in London despite the odds against growing a monster marrow in an inch of soil on the quarter deck. This is known as 'the crusading spirit'. It is the same sentiment which leads boat people to campaign against the juggernauts on the Embankment which runs right past their back doors; for prison reform, which is understandable in the light of Dr Johnson's opinion of boats; and for inclusion within the Rent Act which, for boat people (who are mavericks) is not understandable in any light.

Or are they mavericks? Are they pioneers of the pierhead or weighed down at anchor? Boat people who are neither offshore nor on the sea are neither fish nor fowl, not mainstream but not entirely flotsam and jetsam either. They are exhibitionists. They may not follow the sartorial fashions of the rest of Chelsea and naturally prefer thigh-high Wellies to footless tights. Tri-skates are not great on gangplanks, nor is fancy dress enhanced by mildew. The exhibits of boat people are the boats themselves, which are their full-time jobs no matter where else they may be summarily employed. Such uphill work, combined with a closer contemplation of water than even the rest of the English enjoy, induces a resignation or phlegm which makes their particular masochism even more personally delightful. Moreover, boat people possess an instinctive knowledge of how to deal with the licensing laws. It is a well-known adage on board any boat that somewhere in the world the sun has always just gone over the yardarm. That is why the seltzers never stop flowing in Chelsea Reach, even when the tide is out.

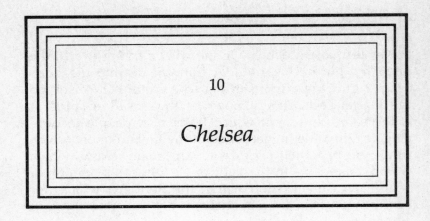

10

Chelsea

IT IS THE ambition of a great many young and not so young things to live, in the words of the song from *Cabaret*, in two sordid rooms in Chelsea. It is the ambition of others to own a darling little white-washed *pied-à-terre* there and fill it with bijou Victorian knick-knacks.

On the face of things Chelsea appears to have a split personality, but underneath their chosen exteriors, Chelsea people share one thing: they have no interior. Underneath the tinsel, as they once said of Hollywood, there is but more tinsel. Chelsea people live by their appearances, and for them. They are hell-bent on drawing attention to themselves. The main thing is to be seen to be having a good time, which is not necessarily the same thing as having one. Chelsea currency is people. Chelsea-ites are very sociable. The pubs and the wine bars, the markets and the streets, the *boutiques* and the clubs are full of people who do not know each other and are trying to remedy the fact. Chelsea people need no introduction, apart from the idea that they are in Chelsea. Outrageous behaviour is perfectly appropriate. Pints of beer are poured down *décolletés* and naughty stories turn the heads of total strangers.

Chelsea people are imaginative. They enjoy squalor

because they imagine it is decadent and they get a *frisson* from the immodest approach. They know all the names of the decadent figureheads of the past, all the *grandes horizontales*, the *bons viveurs*, the weirdos, dissidents and freaks, but the name is about all they know. Hampstead people, who are *literati*, know all about everything, which is why they are so afraid of it. Chelsea people know nothing at all so they have nothing at all to worry about. Chelsea people are flighty and fickle. They find knowledge ponderous and ignorance charming, or the appearance of it. Even if they work hard they do not like to be seen working hard, for they want to give the impression that they are so brilliant they don't have to work at all. They are not in the least bit interested in scoring a proper education. They are not interested in diplomas or qualifications. They leave school as soon as possible unless it is art school. They never go to university unless it is the Sorbonne. They are not interested in the past or what it can teach them, or the future and what it may or may not hold. They are only interested in the present and what they are going to do about it. They never read books because it is too much like hard work, but they devour magazines and gossip is their favourite hobby alongside dressing up. They know what they should be wearing and talking about this week because they read it in the magazines, and they know what anybody who is anybody should be doing. This is called being *avant-garde*. There is a French word for almost every facet of Chelsea life. This is called being cultured.

Formal culture is not important in Chelsea. Chelsea people rarely go to the theatre, the opera or a concert. The Royal Court, though it may be situated on the edge of Chelsea, is not full of Chelsea people. It is full of Hampstead people visiting Chelsea for a peep at *la vie de bohème*. Chelsea people, unlike Hampstead people, are not *voyeurs*. They are do-eurs, triers and fliers. They find it hard to sit still through other people's performances and any pause in the action sends them rushing to the nearest bar. Chelsea people put on better productions in their homes than they will ever see at any theatre. Some of the great party-givers and goers live in Chelsea. Their *soirées* are legendary. They like name-dropping and make-up and masked balls and all forms of artifice. They all want to be astonished all of the time, which makes Chelsea people very exhausting to spend time with. They like late nights and late mornings and lots of licence and some of them like specialised forms of entertainment which are safer indulged behind closed doors. Two Chelsea people together constitutes a party, three is liable to provoke an orgy—or at least that is what Chelsea people would have you think. Chelsea people enjoy shocking other people, but they don't enjoy being criticised for it. They are guiltless and guileless and, though open to any experience, strangely, attractively innocent. Other people call this eccentric. Chelsea people want everyone to love them. They like to see their names in newspapers so they know that they exist, and they employ cuttings services to tell them what they have been doing lately.

Chelsea people rarely leave Chelsea—partly because it is very difficult to find any public transport west of Sloane Square. They are locked by their bend of the river into their own particular madness which they call art. ART. Chelsea people are very artistic. Whichever sex they are (which is sometimes difficult to tell) they like flower-arranging and hairdressing and crocheted sweaters and designer jewellery. They like baubles of any kind even if they can only afford a safety pin through the ear. They like body paint and hair dye, they mould their tresses into improbable sculptures and whether they are skinheads or Sloane Rangers they paint on a personality which immediately indicates their tastes. They are magpies and they are attracted to everything that glitters. They collect glittering witticisms and bitchinesses about their ex-lovers and they collect pictures which look like they were drawn by Bacon or Cocteau but not necessarily were. Chelsea art is rarely permanently enshrined on Chelsea walls. Chelsea is changeable, Chelsea is a life-class.

Whereas Hampstead people pride themselves on their completely realistic hold on life, Chelsea people would never admit to having a realistic hold on anything. They know the fantasy life is far preferable to the real one, which is why they like drugs when they can get them and alcohol when they can't. Chelsea people are rarely endangered by their indulgences. They are much more endangered by the *bourgeoisie*. They are more honest than their commercial counterparts in Covent Garden and more canny than their trendy counterparts in Notting Hill. Chelsea people are cannier than they look. They shop at stores which are never knowingly undersold and at cash-and-carries once a month because essential shopping is so boring. They window shop all the time and acquire ideas they could never buy. They can run up ball gowns out of old curtains, or, better still, they know how to find someone else who can. If they are broke they know how to live off someone else who is not. Chelsea people put on a brave face even if they are poor. It is no great shakes going back to a lonely bedsitter somewhere like Oakley Street night after night. Chelsea people rarely go back to their bedsitters alone, but they are usually left alone after half an hour or so. This is the part of London where television actors and advertising agents, peers of the realm and ambidextrous interior designers keep their mistresses. Often they are not very generous with them. The mistresses may be rather sorrowful creatures but they are basically very hopeful. Any mistress who is still a mistress by the age of thirty has rationalised that she is saving herself for a millionaire.

Chelsea people are distinguished by their dreams and they would not be typical without them. On the whole, they would rather be notorious than famous because fame sounds too much like hard work. Every photographer imagines that he will one day wake up to find he is Cecil Beaton, every writer to find she is Colette. Every Chelsea attic holds a would-be Quentin Crisp, every studio a would-be Augustus John and every little waitress wants to be his would-be model. Chelsea people know a little about genuine artists because of the time they spent in art school when they couldn't think of anything else to do. Besides, Whistler and Turner and John all once lived in Chelsea and there are plaques on the houses to say so. Chelsea people capitalise on their associations. These days John's studio is rented out for rather staid socialite parties where everybody is thrilled to be in Chelsea even if they know none of the other guests. The guests are likely to be naughty girls from good families, who gravitate to Chelsea for their social life though they might not actually live there. They have lots of confidence, yet they do badly paid jobs for publishing houses and glossy magazines. They may wear green hair or footless tights or they may wear Hermes headscarves and Gucci shoes—but either way they have very loud voices and extravagant opinions of themselves. A lot of them have been to convent school. Convent school is an almost certain recipe for a misspent after-life. Once upon a time these little *communicantes* would have been *débutantes*. In the 'Fifties, Chelsea was full of *débutantes* announcing to the world that they were having a wonderful time. The Chelsea set included Princess Margaret and other gay young things who could afford to be defiant of convention. In the 'Sixties everyone could afford to do away with convention. *Débutantes* refused to be *débutantes* and started out life instead as petrol pump attendants. They married rich men who pulled in in Jaguars and later on they had noisy divorces. Then they went back to being petrol pump attendants, or *boutique* assistants or barmaids. They are still today's Chelsea set.

Old hell-raisers never give up, they simply join the Chelsea Arts Club. This Chelsea meeting place was resuscitated by leading Chelsea lights and five years ago they even managed to resuscitate the Chelsea Arts Ball, that legendary annual showplace of Chelsea *moeurs* and fashions which used to fill the Albert Hall. These days things have changed, but that doesn't stop Chelsea people ardently pursuing their legends. Chelsea people are story-tellers and if the facts don't fit their anticipations they simply make them up.

One resident—who has made Chelsea his base since his teens—first arrived in Chelsea by chance. Chance always plays a leading role in Chelsea life. He was hitching a lift from his parents' home in the country when he was picked up by a typical Chelsea girl driving to her parents' flat off the King's Road. He liked it so much he stayed. When he married he moved to The Boltons (which would rather be thought of as being Chelsea than Earl's Court) and when he married again he found a new house just a couple of streets away. His friends in the area are cartoonists and painters. In the old days they used to meet at pubs like the Admiral Codrington and the Queen's Elm—'Very dull now. I have to admit that livening up the Arts Club is rather like cycling through molasses. It used to be the great spot for reprobates. You could always find a friend underneath the snooker table. These days we have to allow even the women to play snooker, otherwise they won't let us leave the house.' So these days the club is rather familial, which is very alarming to sentimental

hard-core Chelsea-ites anxious to protect the place's reputation from the twin perils of old age and respectability. If
they can't find any action in Chelsea they take a cab to
Soho where they always used to fall readily among like-
minded ravers and *raconteurs*. These days, however, even
Soho is full of people from Brixton.

The fact is that, sooner or later, even ravers and
raconteurs slow down. The Chelsea housewife is liable to
be rather correct on the surface of things. She pretends she
has put away her past and becomes obsessed with lace
tablecloths and *vol-au-vent* cases. But she is unlikely to
have given up her bad ways entirely. She has affairs on
the side and sometimes she has affairs with women. This
is not because she particularly likes women but because it
titillates the men. Chelsea families arrange their affairs
round school hours. Unlike Hampstead people, Chelsea
people do not do it in front of the children, or *'pas devant
les enfants'* as they say in Chelsea. In the old days of help in
the house, married people strayed between five and seven
when the servants were preparing dinner. Now they stray
between eleven and one. This is when the kids are in
school, the *au pair* is in English class and even the idlest
Chelsea husband is on his way to work, or to the Chelsea
Arts Club.

Chelsea people never confess. Even if they find each
other *in flagrante delicto* they will lie their way out rather
than make a clean breast of things. They will probably say
they were giving artificial respiration to the milkman or
teaching life-saving to the *au pair* so she can take the
children on a safe holiday. They never refer to the incident
again though their partners will find a way of getting their
own back. A favourite way is to go off and have an affair
with the guilty party's best friend. They will make sure
they are caught once again in the act and then strenuously
deny the rumour that they cannot be trusted. Chelsea

people find this game-playing a lot of fun and as a result of it everything at home is sweetness and light. The Chelsea housewife brings her husband his martini on a silver tray when he comes home and embroiders his initials on slippers which she has had made in Harrods. She is perfectly capable of knocking up a *cordon bleu* meal because she has usually taken a *cordon bleu* course somewhere between art classes and the Sorbonne. She is a marvellous coper. She hires and fires *au pairs* without a murmur and will abandon the dog under a passing truck if he pees in the aspidistra.

Chelsea people do not send their children to state schools if they can help it, though this does not mean that they have any more respect for their offspring's education than they did for their own. What it means is that the school run is one of the great events in the life of a Chelsea wife. It is a social event and therefore must be conducted in the best possible circles. Kensington people and Knightsbridge people conduct such a social event impeccably. Chelsea people must be seen to put a spanner in the works. Once a week, when it is her turn to do the school run, the Chelsea wife will fling her St Laurent raincoat over her protruding Janet Reger nightie and drive her own and everyone else's children off to Lady Eden's or to Eaton House or to the French Lycée in her run-around black Renault '*Le Car*'. There she will parade herself before a lot of other mothers in couture raincoats with or without nighties at the wheels of a lot of continental cars. Some mothers drive very large Mercedes, some mothers drive Volkswagens, but all of them drive very badly indeed. They all wear dark glasses and the language to be heard in the traffic jams outside the school is more educational than anything that goes on inside it. Chelsea fathers also do the school run because no one in Chelsea wants to be seen to be predictable. Chelsea fathers behave very aggressively towards other Chelsea fathers and even tear the wind-screen wipers off each other's Mercedes.

Chelsea people may have rotten manners themselves but they expect their undisciplined children to have excellent manners, at least when they are in their company. This is because it makes life a lot easier for the parents. Often they send them away to boarding school so they can concentrate more fully on having their own fun. Chelsea wives do not always insist on custody of their children in divorce, which is often the fate of a Chelsea marriage despite all the protestations of total fidelity. Chelsea people get divorced when things are no longer fun. The lack of inherent fun is why they do not always press for custody. Chelsea people like children because they are young and pretty, but they know they are not as interesting as grown-ups. They also know that their children will have their own time soon enough, so their parents do not waste their own youth upon them while they could be doing something else with it. But the children have their uses. Chelsea children expect to go abroad during their holidays. Enterprising Chelsea mothers, therefore, arrange to take them on educational trips to Switzerland or Italy while their husbands are still back home. At the same time they arrange for their lovers to take their own children on holiday to the same places in Switzerland or Italy. These holidays are like French farces and are very exhausting, which means that Chelsea wives always have to have another holiday, without the children but under the same circumstances.

In the meantime they languish a lot around the house in lovely little Victorian *negligés* smelling of *sal volatile* and *tisane*. Chelsea housewives never do a job outside marriage because it is far too exhausting organising the marriage. Often this cannot be done without prescribed drugs and Chelsea wives always have doctors they call by their first names. They usually have several doctors and can manage one way or another to get a prescription for absolutely anything they think they need. In this way they are like French housewives. If French housewives got on with any other housewives they would get on with Chelsea ones.

Chelsea people like Paris and the South of France and unlike Hampstead people they despise all the uninteresting bits in between, except for the wine-tasting regions. They always know someone with a *château* in Champagne, a yacht on the Riviera or a flat in the Latin *quartier*. They always stay in a different *château*, flat or on a different yacht. This way they never have to pay their way. They speak fluent French with atrocious accents and they don't give a damn what the French think about that. They don't give a damn what anyone thinks. They are not religious and they are not atheists, they simply do not care. They think life is too short to worry about things like that. They don't care about politics either, but this does not stop them taking up politics as a profession. They like the attention and they like the game-playing.

On their death-beds Chelsea people remember their convent educations. They have nothing to lose and all their lives they have aimed both to have their cake and to eat it too.

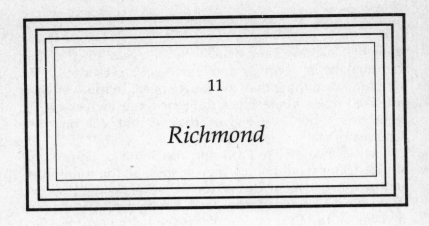

11

Richmond

RICHMOND IS A very charming London suburb which could lie miles away from the capital city. It could lie as far away as Germany, whose provincial towns it greatly resembles and whose inhabitants were amongst its foremost pioneers. German princelings and Princesschens who intermarried with our Royalty loved to choose it for their residences because they felt so at home there. Queen Mary brought up her family in Richmond Park, and such superior connections no doubt account for the fierce loyalty of its residents. It is so attractive to the people who live there that they scarcely ever leave it unless they absolutely have to. Unlike Clapham people—who would have no use for Clapham if it were not right over Chelsea Bridge—Richmond people are insular about Richmond, and if it were cut off by a tidal wave from central London they would not mourn the bright lights at all. Some Richmond people manage to spend a whole lifetime there without ever once experiencing any curiosity about the world outside; some of them have never even been as far as Hyde Park Corner. They never speak about the convenience of the District Line or the Southern Railway or the 33 bus or the South Circular Road, all of which are perfectly poised to commute them wherever they need to go. They speak about *their* Green, and *their* theatre, *their* local restaurants with *their* home-made apple pie, and *their* river, which, by some irony, is the same river which flows past that other seat of power the Houses of Parliament.

Richmond people play in Richmond and they work there. Since there are a lot of actors in Richmond they are also out of work there. Richmond, with its park and its playing fields, its water meadows and formal gardens, its church socials and its pottery classes, its dog-walking and its horse-riding, not to mention its idle boating, is the perfect playground. It is a far healthier playground than Chelsea, which is sometimes thought to be the play-ground of London. It lacks the fumes, the fans, the fun and the frissons. Richmond people are not frivolous like Chelsea people. They are upright and respectable and still think of Richmond not so much as a suburb but as a country town. But Richmond people are not country people. The nearest they ever come to blood sports is knocking down one of the Queen's deer in the Royal park by accident with the family Volvo.

Some people no longer use the park, seeing it as a vulgar Sunday trap where you are more likely to come across a traffic jam than in Trafalgar Square. People who think like this do not jog in it or picnic in it or gravitate towards it for long, lusty nature walks. They play discreet games of squash in their lunch hours instead, moving backwards and forwards from the sports centre to the wine bar. Such people suffer a high mortality rate from heart attacks on court or in the changing rooms, but such things are only whispered about in Richmond which does not like to be seen in any bad light. Richmond people like discreet dramas. They do not run round in small circles drawing attention to themselves, they wait to be dis-covered, hiding their lights meanwhile virtuously under so many bushels. This does not mean that Richmond

people are modest. On the contrary they are as pleased
with themselves as Punch. They are absolutely confident
that they have found the true path to happiness—which is
to eat wholemeal bread, drink cider, serve lentil soup off
placemats depicting the Star and Garter, have children on
scholarships to fee-paying schools and collect obscure first
editions.

Richmond is known as Hampstead-on-Thames, but
Richmond people are far more secure than Hampstead
people, though there is a touch of the crofter about both of
them. Richmond people will not necessarily bore you with
their virtues until you ask for it. Watch out if you do.
Whereas Hampstead people all hold exactly the same
views on exactly the same subjects (which may therefore
be avoided), Richmond people have much more obscure
information at their fingertips which they are dying to
unleash. Whereas Hampstead people are liberals who
disapprove of everything, Richmond people are dyed-in-
the-wool reactionaries and have to be drawn out by
someone in apparent agreement with them. Such defensive reticence means that Richmond people would get off to
a slow start if they did not order in the entertainment for
the occasion. Saturday night is party night in Richmond.
Richmond people never go downtown on Saturday night
except to bash the skinheads, queers and Mohicans who
come over the defences from such down-market places as
Hounslow, Staines and Isleworth to try to gatecrash their
parties. They also come to disco, drink and ogle at the
Auberge, which was once a coffee bar where Mick Jagger
had his first success. Richmond people do not trust people
who come from Hounslow, Staines and Isleworth because
of this, unless they are wearing uniform and serving
drinks on British Airways.

Richmond people trust uniforms. They are patriotic and
hearty. Once the first barrel of mead is downed there is no

stopping them. This is the moment they can effortlessly remember all the names of all the Welsh Internationals who ever attempted to score tries at Twickenham Rugby Football Ground since 1935; or all the weights of all the Magdalene coxes since the Boer War. Ask a Richmonder a question about the Boat Race, the Succession, the War or the Stock Market and he may well never stop answering it. This means that quite successful Richmond conversations take place between two people speaking at the same time on quite different subjects of obscure expertise without paying the slightest attention to the other. The same goes for the girls. One lady expert on glass-blowing might encounter another on hand-blocked textiles. A bookseller might discourse happily on the third Indo-European vowel change while his friend simultaneously translates Viking drinking songs. Such Richmond people think this is intellectual, but deep down in their heart of hearts they know it is encyclopaedic. As long as they have read it somewhere in print, written by someone else (preferably with letters after his name), they believe it implicitly. Richmond people know everything about houses and gardens, and what they know is that they must be tidy. Their furniture is arranged round the edge of their rooms, their flowers round the edge of their lawns. Their edges are trimmed, their daffs dead-headed, their fences creosoted, their gutters clean, their eaves mended, their branches lopped, their leaves swept up the moment they fall from the tree. Their ashes are thrown out the moment they fall from their cigarettes. In November, the Richmond air is thick with the smoke of Richmond bonfires, and in December there is always a pair of gardening gloves around the Christmas tree. Richmond people complain a lot about the smoke from other people's bonfires and the shade from other people's overhanging trees.

Pour a Richmond housewife a sherry and she will tell you all she has learned from Percy Thrower. She will tell you all about cutting and grafting and pruning and training, trailing and weeping and rambling and feeding and spraying and watering and sowing and shading. Pour her a gin and she will start on her top soil and her loam, her humus, her dung, her mulch and her sequestrian. Pour her two and you will get the entire wisdom of Arthur Negus plus a free appraisal of the reproduction Sheraton drinks cabinet in the corner. Richmond wives rarely work. They have hobbies. They do post-natal work and grow monster marrows for garden fêtes and flog pots of homemade jam for charity. On summer Saturdays vicarage gardens are full of young couples manning the tombola and taking pot luck on the Snoopy dip. On Thursday afternoons the church halls are full of basket-weaving classes. Young married ladies may be seen at all times in Burberry macs at the wheels of estate wagons filled with children, Labradors and antique furniture, which gives further rise to Royal rumours. On Sundays their husbands take the children in the same estate wagons to pick up the *Observer* from newsagents who would be quite willing to deliver. This is because Richmond husbands aim to end up in the pub. Richmond pubs have lines of children outside them answering to names like Vanessa and James, wearing striped dungarees and yellow Wellies, eating crisps and drinking Coke.

Given that the park has become too proletarian these days, it is naturally the aim of every Richmond person to own a house overlooking the river, which is at its most metropolitanly sylvan at this spot. Whereas Richmond people who overlook the river are condemned to enjoy the view of the multi-storey carparks, the skating rinks and the warehouses of Twickenham from the terraces of their beautiful eighteenth-century houses, Twickenham people get to enjoy the view of the beautiful eighteenth-century houses. Richmond people who make it a point never to cross their bridge never see this view themselves. This means that they will pay absolutely anything for a print of the view to hang in their drawing room so they can enjoy it too. Or even a placemat of it which they will conceal beneath their plate of Sunday roast beef. (Richmond people can still afford Sunday roast beef.) There are a great many print-sellers, print-makers, print-restorers and placemat makers in Richmond who flog views of all sorts of Georgiana to all sorts of Richmond dwellers. Such a thriving pride is there in Richmond views that one resident who lives on the river himself and can't see them, has set up his own publishing company to reproduce them. This is a no-risk venture since there are many more people in Richmond than are needed to pay for his limited editions. The most lowly terraced Richmond cottage is filled with tinted etchings in black-and-gilt frames of everything from the Palace to that bend in the river which looks down on the country proper.

This is known as Art. Richmond people think of themselves as very artistic, but they paint with their little fingers crooked. Art in Richmond means pottery ashtrays and pressed flowers, pictures of cocker spaniels and Siamese cats with eyes like a Trechikov print. Art can also mean advertising and architecture. Just like Clapham people, Richmond people like to gut the insides of their houses and bring in some popular design company. Since some Richmond houses are worth around a quarter of a million pounds, they are often gutted to contain offices, but a lot of Richmond people are still personally very rich indeed. They live in monumentally well appointed houses and only ever wear jeans and suede shoes. They flaunt their property prices and only ever shop at chain stores. These people are usually television personalities who flock to this part of the world, as do certain bona fide showbiz people who are on their way from Hollywood-on-Thames (Barnes) to Beverly Hills-on-Thames (Windsor, Bray and points west). Richmond wives consequently have mildly indiscreet affairs with people who know people who know people who are something on TV. Their husbands are very proud of this and discreetly tell everybody who does not know already. This means that Richmond children get very confused and, despite their scholarships to expensive day-schools, are likely to grow up not quite all good.

12

Shepherd's Bush

IN SHEPHERD'S BUSH they say that when CAV gets a cold, Shepherd's Bush sneezes. CAV is the local factory. It makes vehicle components. Vehicle components are those parts which go to make up a vehicle which always retain an identity of their own even when they are assembled.

As every car driver knows, it is as important to him to be the proud possessor of a walnut dashboard, triple fin lights or a chrome roller bar as to possess the English Mini, the German Audi or the Japanese Charmant to which these things are attached. Bush people normally buy British, but not very often. Shepherd's Bush cars are usually very old, though they may be driven by quite young men. They are invariably among some of the worst drivers in the country, though occasionally outdone by very old drivers of very new cars, of which there are not very many in Shepherd's Bush. It is not necessary, however, to know the age, still less the identity of a driver, to know whether or not a given car will be well driven. It is enough to look at the registration. Bad drivers have registration numbers ending with the letters C to P or anything after V, and anyone who values his paintwork will scrupulously avoid them particularly on a Sunday afternoon. V cars are sufficiently new for their drivers to be completely unfamiliar with them, over proud and terrified of crashing them in their stage fright. C to P cars are so old that their drivers no longer care if they crash them. They bump them round town as if they were dodgems or stock cars. Drivers with even earlier registrations lovingly maintain them because they are antiquities and swing them round with a confidence that usually leads to good results.

This leaves those drivers with R, S and T plates who are the best drivers of all because they are familiar with their cars and confident but not emotionally attached to them. Shepherd's Bush drivers invariably have number plates ending in something between C and P. The number plates are invariably held on by string. Sometimes they have no number plates. Shepherd's Bush people are not always in a position to buy their own motor car accessories but this does not stop them trading in them.

Car accessories are currency, and somewhere between the airport and the centre of every capital city in the world you will find a decorator row where vehicles may be pulped, pirated and recycled as in Shepherd's Bush. This is a good place to go in search of anything from a slightly used muffler to a second-hand sheepskin seat cosy, a dangling dachshund or personalised name plates for either side of the windscreen advertising that this Vauxhall is the property of BILL and EDNA. It is a good place to go in search of your entire car if it disappears off a side street at night, though you had better be quick about it if there is to be any possibility of finding it. Shepherd's Bush people believe in sharing everything and this includes your possessions and their draught. They know how to turn a trick or two in extremis. They know how to climb a drainpipe, or wield a blunt instrument, or stand beneath a lorry when something useful is about to fall off it. Shepherd's Bush people are nothing if not practical.

They'll handle a nice bit of jewellery if it comes their way, preferably if it is someone else's, but they much prefer a portable video recorder complete with the previous owner's choice of erotic cassettes. Shepherd's Bush people are fond of entertainment. This is obviously because they are ringed by the visible presence of BBC Television: Kensington House on the way to Hammersmith, Lime Grove on the way to Chiswick, the BBC Television Theatre on the Green and the Television Centre on the way to White City. Shepherd's Bush people, whoever they are, are united by their respect for entertainment. The pubs have TV pin-ups on their walls, the caffs have TV pin-ups on their walls, and so do the shoeshops, the tailors, the garages, the flats and the houses. The OAPs like a nightly knees-up in the church hall. The children learn to tap and soft shoe as soon as they can walk and beg their mothers to enroll them in stage school.

In everything else, Bush people (as they call themselves) are divided. On the one hand there are the new estates which stretch from the Uxbridge Road to White City where everyone who is anyone lives off the DHSS, works at CAV and supports QPR. On the other hand there are the old estates between the Uxbridge Road and Hammersmith where everyone who is anyone works as an ASM at the BBC or makes films about UDI and AID. (They are very big on abbreviations at the Bush.) Then there is the hinterland where everyone works at ITN or ATV, has babies at QCH and says they live in Chiswick. Some of those people get published in the *TLS*, gossip to PHS and subscribe to the RSC. They buy prints from the RA, remember lovingly the GPO and universally hate OPEC because they live just that little bit too far out of town to rely on LT with or without the GLC.

A lot of comedians live at the Bush. Bush people are natural comedians which stems from the lively vernacular.

Some of them also make a living at it. Two of the original comedians to operate from the Bush formed a company called ALS, having met in hospital where they both had TB. BBC people wear cable-knits and Hush Puppies, drink gin and tonic in the club, holiday in France and eat escargots at the Balzac Bistro just across the road from the Proustian Albertine Bar. CAV people wear nylon anoraks, drink beer and buy shorts, holiday on the Costa Brava which they call the Costa Lot, and eat pie, eels and mash down the Goldhawk Road. Comedians wear tweeds, drink wine, take 'working' holidays in the Caribbean and eat in town since the demise of Bertorelli's at the Bush. Sometimes they don't bother to eat at all, especially if it is their turn to cook.

Everyone still drinks in the public bars and plays snooker. You can tell an area which is proud of its origins to the point of resisting improvement if it has not yet got round to desegregrating all its pubs. Pubs in Richmond, Barnes and Chelsea are liable to put in floral carpets throughout and hunting horns. Bush people are not interested in hunting horns. They are only interested in the beer being cheap. Bush people like a 'good deal' and they are liable to get just such a thing down the market.

Shepherd's Bush market is the sort of real, practical, honest (well almost), down-to-earth market such as you will not find in Camden Town or Portobello Road or Chelsea these days. You will not see an American for miles unless he is slumming it with a BBC producer looking for local colour. You will see a lot of archetypal Arabs in veils and beaks who know exactly how to operate beneath the tracks because it reminds them of a Middle Eastern bazaar right off the tourist route. Even the goods are the same the world over these days. Thus Arabs from the Hilton and the Dorchester have given up Marks & Spencer's, where their inscrutable buying methods are open to charges of shoplifting, and come down in their limousines to the Goldhawk Road to close a good cash deal on some status symbol like a cabin trunk or a refrigerator to take back to the desert where they have no electricity. Shepherd's Bush market glitters with cheerful baubles and brushed nylon Babygros. You won't find a lot of stripped pine commodes or maplewood picture frames or Victorian nightgowns or used postcards. You won't find a lot of wickerwork plant-holders or ethnic cushions being snapped up by bearded bisexuals wearing baby-slings. You will find a lot of purposeful harassed mothers in curlers wielding see-through prams like battering rams and wrangling over the nylon doilies, quilted housecoats, candlewick bedspreads, nesting tables, bacon sand-wiches, yams, plantains or mangoes or the sex of some companionable puppy to protect them after dark. In Shepherd's Bush market anything with pointed ears is called an Alsatian, anything with a flat face is called a mastiff. Ask for its pedigree and you can be sure you will not be disappointed. Some form of pedigree will be produced together with proof that the pet of your choice has been dewormed, deloused, vaccinated against every known complaint and weaned on iron filings, which makes a burglar's ankle taste like whipped Chantilly.

Bush people are very fussy about their purchases. You cannot put one over on them. You may not find too many Dralon three-piece suites between the covers of *House and Garden*, but they like them. You will not see too many turquoise crimplene frocks in *Vogue*, but Bush people don't care. They pay a lot of attention to their appearance and to their hairstyles. There are more hairdressers in Shepherd's Bush than there are sports shops and there are a lot of both. There are hairstyles in Shepherd's Bush you will never see in Knightsbridge and the names only begin to describe them: fantastic bunnies, big puffs, skin

partings, deluxe discos, afro snakes and top knots, venti-
lated freedoms and yak flick-ups. On the whole the bigger
the better. West Indians who used to have their hair
discreetly straightened while white people had theirs
permed have the confidence these days to wear it twice as
curly. The whites, meanwhile, wear it twice as colourful.
The most glorious coxcombs parade their artifice up in
town. Enforced leisure has persuaded people to enjoy
their differences and not be ashamed of them. The Irish in
the Bush, of whom there are many, enjoy being as
different as possible from each other. Bush newsagents
import not just one Irish newspaper, but nearer twenty.
Tiny Bush children, sent out by sleeping parents, learn to
identify their titles early like comic strips way before they
can read: the *Longford Leader*, the *Leitrim Observer*, the
Drogheda Independent, the *Tipperary Star*, the *Sligo Champion*, the *Connaught Telegraph*, the *Kilkenny People*, the
Kerryman, the *Corkman*.

You would not think to look at the Bush now that a mere
one hundred years ago sheep would safely graze on the
children's playground on the Green. And, as their names
suggest, in Wood Lane, Ealing Common and Wormwood
Scrubs. You might not guess today that it became a health
resort with the best air in the home counties or that
London's smartest racetrack lay upon its boundaries. Bush
people used to follow the horses. Lately they have been
going to the dogs.

Those parts of London which undergo total physical
transformation always seem to retain one strong link with
their past identity. Mayfair is still full of adventuresses,
Notting Hill of artists, Bloomsbury of the literati who these
days work in the up-market press. It is nothing new for
Bush dwellers to live by their wits or to pay the price. A
century ago highwaymen were plundering the coaching

inns which still stand on the Uxbridge Road; two centuries
ago the Bush was a place of public execution; three
centuries ago one Miles Syndercombe rented a thatched
cottage in the middle of Shepherd's Bush Green for the
sole purpose of ambushing Oliver Cromwell, but the
enterprise was ill-starred for Cromwell got there first.
Syndercombe poisoned himself and was buried in the
Tower with a stake driven through his heart. HM Prison at
the Scrubs metes out a relatively gentle punishment
compared to that. Syndercombe's cottage stood at the
Bush until the end of Victorian times. Today the vernacular would have it that there is still a cottage at the Bush,
though it is full of loitering queens, drug addicts, tran-
sients and meths drinkers. Though each compass point is
visible from the others the place gets short shrift from
respectable locals from the side streets. They even extend
their condemnation to the Christmas circus which is
allowed by the local council the dubious favour of camp-
ing there in the mud. Vagrants, mutter the old ladies
walking their plump cereal-fed dogs, travellers whose
smelly menagerie only encourages the filthy pigeons to
foul the footpaths. Bush residents prefer television to any
other form of entertainment. Bush people no longer
actually live at the Bush itself, which is now a shopping
centre. The residential centre has switched to the starchier
area of Starch Green, where those washerwomen who
used to stiffen their clients' collars in the local brook, nowadays enjoy a good malicious gossip in the launderette
while they watch the T-shirts tumble.

13

St John's Wood

IT'S NOT AS easy living in St John's Wood as it looks. It
takes a lot of work to keep up with the Cohens—and the
the El Sauds, the Azizes and the Ewings. All those people
who are compulsively at each others' throats back home
are quite happy to brush fur coats in St John's Wood High
Street. Money is the great leveller. There is a lot of money
in St John's Wood.

You can almost smell the improvement in the air as you
drive across the Regent's Canal. You can't avoid the status
symbols: the Jags and the Mercs, the Polos and the
Caddies and the custom-built, chrome-plated, purple-
pearlised, multiple-exhaust, open-top fun buggies full of
bright young things in tans and leather jackets. The streets
become wider, the gardens bigger, the trees gaudier, the
buildings taller. The flats that look down on the residence
of the American ambassador might appropriately be
looking down on Central Park. Or Miami Beach. St John's
Wood has a lot in common with Miami Beach except for
the sun. This does not stop St John's Wood people
wearing sunglasses. They wear them when it is raining
and they wear them at night. They wear them to buy in
the smoked salmon or to go out to dinner. They wear
black glasses and mirrored glasses, graded glasses and

tinted glasses, smoky glasses and sun-sensitive glasses. They wear them with pink frames and gilt frames and no frames. They wear them in kaleidoscope colours with designer initials and diamanté sprigs. They also wear regular glasses.

St John's Wood people are addicted to all forms of medical care except the National Health Service. Whether they need their teeth straightened or their busts lifted, their thighs filleted or their cheeks tightened, their eyes widened or their wrinkles ironed, their noses cropped, their hair transplanted, their fertility counted or their minds analysed, they know some miracle specialist who can be certain to charge twice as much to do it as the miracle specialist of their nextdoor neighbour. Quite likely he will be their nextdoor neighbour on the other side. Not only will he be maintaining some gorgeous, grandiose neo-Georgian, ante-Bellum, post-Palladian pile with five reception rooms, gilded bath taps and drive-in space for ten cars, but he will also be maintaining the authentic slightly faded Regency ground floor suite in Harley Street. The magazines in the waiting room are back numbers but he's charging double figures to answer the telephone. Patients who have oil wells in their gardens do not trust a doctor who does not have a tennis court at home which he never uses and a swimming pool which gets used once a year. If such patients have an ache they go in for observation, if they have a pain they have everything out. This is an irresistible subject for discussion at the local pâtisserie or outside the mosque. St John's Wood people, who are overweight, do not first discuss the treatment they have been having, they discuss the food they had while they were having the treatment. St John's Wood people go into private clinics to avoid National Health food.

If they are pregnant they go into the Avenue Clinic.

Naked St John's Wood people may come into the world, but naked they do not stay for long. Before they have left the clinic they have a wardrobe full of French designer clothes and a canteen of silver for their dowry. They have their first hair-cut at Leonard's in Mayfair and their first car in good time for their seventeenth birthday. Along the way they will have acquired braces on their teeth—which are then capped because of the grooves made by the braces. This is the part of London where you will find endless fashionable thirteen-year-olds defaced by endless fashionable specialists to have them grow up into endless identically fashionable adults. St John's Wood children are cloned by orthodontics and plastic surgery among their other addictions to American fashions. They wear sneakers in the streets and shoelaces in their hair and baseball caps over the shoelaces and Sony earphones over the baseball caps and they spend a compulsory four days a year in Disney World in Orlando. This is because their parents have invariably bought into a little concrete condominium somewhere in Florida along with a lot of other St John's Wood parents. Or a little concrete condominium in Marbella, or a little concrete condominium in Nice. All the mothers gather at the condominiums as soon as school is out, leaving all the fathers to sell more burglar alarms, or real estate, or soft toys to pay for all the brocade furnishings in the condominiums, the slimming salads and all the duty-free Maneschewitz they can drink. In the summer they pay for the obligatory outings to MicMac and Tetou and the portable gold American Express card in case the bikini they bought at Brown's is out of fashion by the time it gets back to the place it was first thought of.

St John's Wood children from private schools all over London and from boarding schools all over the Home Counties converge on Florida every Christmas and Easter. They all come back with all the latest American hardware and software to flaunt before all the children who do not live in St John's Wood. They have pocket calculators and their own video libraries as well as the latest Blondie records and Snoopy lunchpacks. All the girls who wanted to be Charlie's Angels last year, now want to be Pamela Ewing. All the boys who now want to be JR used to want to be Woody Allen. Most of them have the eyeglasses. St John's Wood people wear pink plastic chains around their necks attached to their glasses to make sure they are never separated from them.

St John's Wood people never do anything more active than driving or shopping or go any place more ethnic than the nudist pool at the Eden Roc, or the Gucci boutique in Old Bond Street. They wear their jewellery in the pool, and their definition of a useful watch is one you can wear in the bubble bath. In the winter they charter small yachts off Key Largo and watch the crew catch small sharks. They are photographed on the shore with pickled bigger ones. St John's Wood people have a lot of photographs taken. They like accessories. They have contact lenses to go with the right hairdo and all the right handbags to go with all the right boots to go with all the right bangles, scarves, hats and dogs. St John's Wood dogs are very small. St John's Wood dogs are smaller than cats. They snap at your ankles and trip you up when they are not lying on *eau-de-nil* eiderdowns with mauve bows in their shampooed locks recovering from a custom clipping at the canine beauty parlour. St John's Wood dogs are chihuahuas and butterflies and poodles and Yorkies who are usually incontinent and have names like Jewel and Spaghetti which reflect their owners' priorities. Their owners are into flash and food and the trappings of culture. They give their children stereos for their fifth birthdays and have grand pianos in the living room whether or not anybody can play them. They collect pictures without glass which sometimes look as if they might be famous and always match the wallpaper. They have throwaway pot plants which are the logical end of conspicuous consumption.

St John's Wood people consume cold cuts and hot coffee, and when they are not shopping in the boutique they are shopping in the delicatessen. St John's Wood freezers are full of garlic bread and gefillte fish and halva and cheesecake in case some relative should drop by and suspect they have no garlic bread, gefillte fish, halva or cheesecake. St John's Wood people walk their dogs as far as the delicatessen and then they walk them back again. Some people who do not have dogs walk empty rhinestone dog-collars instead. This is an American custom designed to eliminate the guilt attached to any pointless pursuit such as simply walking for its own enjoyment. There is a lot of guilt in St John's Wood as well as a lot of gilt. St John's Wood people walk their dogs in order to meet other people walking their dogs in order to kwetch on the street corner about all the other people they are lucky enough not to meet. It is always pointless for the dogs to meet each other since they are inevitably wearing quite as many clothes as their owners.

St John's Wood people like embellishment. They never wear one ring when they can wear ten, they never wear their hair brown when they can dye it blonde or wear it blonde when they can rinse it blue. The hairdressing salon is the cultural centre of St John's Wood. Even the men have their hair blow-dried. Whereas Clapham people clean the house for the arrival of the cleaning lady, St John's Wood people do their hair in order to go down to the hairdressers. Invariably they cover their hairdos as soon as they have them with pastel pink synthetic scarves. When their hair is dirty they go to the massage parlour and when they have been massaged they go back to the hairdresser.

St John's Wood hairdos are very buoyant and very derivative. St John's Wood people are very derivative. Go into a St John's Wood restaurant any night except Friday and you would swear you were sitting next to Bette Midler, if not Omar Sharif. Across the way someone very like Neil Diamond will be having dinner with someone very like Barbra Streisand. A Lew Grade will be dining a Marcia Williams along with most of Harold Wilson's Honours List. In the corner there may be the odd Einstein with or without a Cat Stevens. St John's Wood people make an effort to look like such people and many others. They are very interested in fame as well as fortune and if they cannot get to know the famous at least they can get to look like them. Some St John's Wood people make an effort to get to know them. They lie in wait for them outside Abbey Road recording studios and collect autographs on behalf of their nephews and nieces. They invite them to their parties to meet all their friends in the rag trade or in import-export somewhere in the Middle East. They give them discounts in their boutiques and wangle themselves invitations to go with them down to a basement in Jermyn Street called Tramp which is run by a nice St John's Wood boy. Tramp, when it is full, is full of St John's Wood boys, which is not necessarily true of other London discotheques which are full of faggots.

St John's Wood is macho, not masochistic. It is futuristic, not nostalgic. St John's Wood boys have no interest in parodying Evelyn Waugh or Christopher Isherwood or anything else that happened in the past. They have no interest in punk or the new Romanticism or any other brief manifestations of the present. What they want is solid and eternal and with any luck they intend to get it. They wear silk shirts open to the navel with many gold chains, while crosses, ankhs, Magen Davids and the hand of Fatimah mingle together for good measure in the hair on their chests. They drive their Porsches to the sun and require little more of their girlfriends than that they have their teeth capped, their hair bleached and keep absolutely stumm in the front seat. St John's Wood blades are not interested in honing their own minds, never mind those of their female accoutrements. They have no time for current affairs. If they read the newspapers they begin at the stock market prices. As far as they are concerned Robin Day is a local estate agent. They do a little dabbling in real estate during the week and at the weekends they go home with their laundry for a plate of chicken soup, humus or clam chowder.

St John's Wood people never stray far from their mother's apron strings. People who do not live in St John's Wood are quite envious of all this solidarity. They are called St John's Wood-bes, and one of the best ways of achieving their ambition is to make a good marriage.

14

Muswell Hill

SOME PEOPLE MAY think it self-evident that Muswell Hill lies on a hill, and therefore hardly worth a mention. This is not the case at all. There are hills and hills and the nature of the hill indicates the nature of the life which can be expected on that hill. Primrose Hill is such a gentle gradient that Primrose Hill residents are only imperceptibly intellectually superior to their neighbours on the flatlands of St John's Wood. Richmond Hill has a rural view and Richmond residents boast of their rural life while clinging to the urbanity of their eighteenth-century residences. Hampstead residents have a huge and dominating vista of the metropolis and they are hugely dominating to all things metropolitan. Blackheath's view is elegant and historical and Blackheath people would like to think of themselves as both these things. Sydenham Hill is the watershed between downtown sophistication and the vulgarity of suburban Kent, and Sydenham residents vacillate between vulgarity and sophistication.

Muswell Hill is a sudden hill. It is a series of sudden hills which yield sudden views one moment and end in sudden impasses the next. A dramatic *camera obscura* on all of London gives way to a burnt-out shell of Ally Pally, the hollow remnant of a local dream. Muswell Hill people take their tone from their hill. They have a certain perspective on life but they do not necessarily get very far with it. They are stuck betwixt and between and finally focused in upon their own minor eccentricities.

In Clapham, Barnes and Fulham, where all the land is flat, people are locked eyeball to eyeball in their daily competitive round: pruning the roses, cleaning the Volvo and painting their stucco this year's choice of cream. Their Edwardian terraces face each other in perfect formation like rival teams in *Come Dancing*. People who live in such perfect formation are bound to conform. On a shallow hill the environment changes gently, and so does the perception of the residents on each successive gradient. But on a steep hill like Muswell Hill one person's outlook may differ radically from the next's. On a steep hill it is impossible to build rows and rows of conformist houses. Even Edwardian terraces may only cling to each other as the contours of the land allow. Muswell Hill terraces are non-conformist. Muswell Hill houses are gingerbread gothic. They have turret rooms and irregular façades, burgeoning balconies, crazy conservatories and multiply-orientated windows. They may be joined to each other at the hip or at the head, and the relationship of each house to the next and to the particular slope it occupies, alters the relationship of its occupants towards the outside world. People who live in straight lines move in tandem, people who live at tangents move at tangents.

This is known as the law of topographical imperative and it is amply demonstrated in Muswell Hill. The high ground of north London is a haven for all sorts of motley refugees who have in common with one another the idea that they have found a jumping off place which has London in its sights but which is not strictly of London, as they are not strictly of each other. Greeks, Rastafarians, Pakistanis, Italians, some English and many students move gradually up its slopes as they acquire the wherewithal to relocate. This is all very well but they are still nowhere in particular. Muswell Hill is neither up nor down. Muswell Hill residents imagine they would love to live in Highgate or Hampstead if only they could rustle up the extra hundred thousand pounds. They look happily back on Harringay and Hornsey for the fact that they do not still live there. They read in their family kitchens both the *Hornsey Journal* which gives a hysterical account of local rape, arson and murder and theft, and the 'Ham and High' with its clever campaigns for cultural centres for gifted widows and infant violin virtuosos.

In fact they do not understand the austerity of either place. They are neither austerely aggressive nor austerely intellectual. They do not know whether they are trendy or traditional. In this Muswell Hill people resemble San Francisco people who also live on a series of abrupt hills. San Francisco people are both brazen and nooky. They claim the highest percentage of queers in any city in the known world, but the fact is their queers are also the most domesticated. Though San Francisco has its share of street life, it has more than its share of unorthodox marriages. San Francisco revels in its heady views: a glimpse here of a spar of the Golden Gate, a glimpse there of Alcatraz, a peep at Coit's Tower from the loo, a smidgen of Nob's Hill from the attic. Muswell Hill has fewer international landmarks, fewer sexual aberrations, but the same sort of pioneer pretensions within old-fashioned perimeters. Muswell Hill people forgo Oxbridge and go to redbrick universities. They get married, not in floorlength white but in floorlength Laura Ashley gowns. They are churchgoers, but they have a penchant for nonconformist churches: Baptists, Spiritualists, Quakers, Methodists, Presbyterians, Reformists, Evangelists, and multiple other schisms congregate on the slopes of Muswell Hill. They are partygoers but they dance to country music rather than the latest sound. If they are in show business there is something quaintly fundamental about their images.

Bona fide Muswell Hill people are egotistical but not all that vain. Their kids do not wear their hair pink, their matrons do not dye theirs blue. They spend their money on clothes, but on the wrong clothes. Their suits are shiny, their coats are weatherproof. They dress their children like grown-ups and their grown-ups like children. They carry their babies around in slings and everyone wears utility outfits as soon as they can walk. Muswell Hill people spoil their children and their children often disappoint them. Muswell Hill children have their own bookshop and their own toyshop full of the sort of toys which are not so much fun as self-improving. They go to good Hampstead schools and more often than not they learn bad manners. Whereas Hampstead children and Islington children are a mere reflection of their parents' egos; whereas Islington mothers have their own bookshop and hope to see their daughters grow into their own feminist image, Muswell Hill mothers are very indulgent of their families. They nanny their own children. They are homebound and happy to be so.

Home is a powerful word in Muswell Hill. Building societies vying with loan plans alternate with home improvement centres in the shopping arcades. Muswell Hill people spend money on their mortgages and on the inside of their houses. They are not particularly interested in smart exteriors. They do not look at their own houses, still less at other people's—if they look out at all, all they have eyes for is the view. They do not spend money on their gardens. They do not trim the borders or plan the rockeries, or plant the snapdragons or even the vege-tables. They hate mowing the lawn, they would rather sandpaper the floor. This is not to say that they dislike plants. They love plants but they do not like them growing outdoors. Muswell Hill people bring their gardens inside and hang them in macramé baskets in the bathroom next to the rack full of do-it-yourself magazines containing handy hints on wheel-changing, paper-hanging, door-stripping, child-care, home-made wines and cuddly felt animals.

There is no limit to the sort of things Muswell Hill people put in their houses. They lack cohesion, but not imagination. They are unlikely to paint their rooms white and dot them sparsely with Italian furniture as they do in Chelsea. They won't choose Regency stripes and repro-duction Chippendale as they do in Barnes, nor multiply-patterned chintz and horse-brasses as they do in Rich-mond. Muswell Hill people will sleep on the floor or in a hammock if they see fit. They love textured accessories: basketwork lampshades, reed wastepaper baskets, asbes-tos tiles, cork walls, hessian, flock, brick or linen. They like their cushions knitted, crocheted, embroidered, woven tapestried, appliquéd, printed, velvet or velour. Their ashtrays are moons, shells, hands, washbasins, swans or toilet bowls. They like streaked glass and mugs with labels like 'The Guv'nor', 'Best Mum' and 'Chief Cook and Bottlewasher', which is the sort of naïve art favoured by any other first generation settlers. They like executive toys, scented candles and such useless artefacts as permeable brollies and see-through screens. Their spending is conspicuous but not distinguished. They have no really grand ambition in sight. They are not agitants even when they try—but this does not stop them from trying. The corporate identity of Muswell Hill, the point at which the peaks get lowered and the flats begin to peak, is the petition. Muswell Hill people will petition about anything even if they do not really want it, or they will petition against if they do. They petition to close roads, to open cinemas, and not to have a tube station even though they have some of the slowest bus routes in London.

All this goes back to 1968. That was the year that anything at all was possible on the continent of Europe. In Paris the philosophies of Karl Marx, Herbert Marcuse and an entire seminary of nineteenth-century precursors bubbled up once more in the shape of the student revolt. In Germany barricades were stormed. Europe was awash with tear gas, bombs, fire and death. Governments teetered. In Hornsey Art School, just down the road from Muswell Hill, an occasional technician locked himself into a lavatory in protest against some obscure clause in a supplementary benefit brochure. Hornsey, not a million miles away from the Highgate Cemetery where Marx is buried, took it upon itself to lead the London student revolt, and distinguished itself by making a collection of the posters, books and similar detritus of this meaningful revolution. It was indeed a golden age and one which the residents of the slopes of this semi-Parnassus have not forgotten, though their art school has disappeared, nominally at least, into some corporate legislature which they despise. These days Muswell Hill people are turning their pioneering sights towards the future of Alexandra Palace. And, as non-conformists, at least they are agreed on one objective: that whatever proposal is put forward for the use of the space, the important thing is always to veto it.

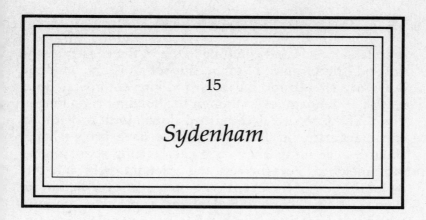

15

Sydenham

SYDENHAM PEOPLE ARE apt proudly to announce in the middle of any conversation that the world's first motor car accident took place on their territory. They rarely add that nothing so exciting ever happens in Sydenham these days. Sydenham minds are obsessed with the past because it took rather more notice of them than the present. They will quote all manner of history and lay claim to a number of bona fide historical firsts, and a number which are almost certainly less credible. Sydenham had the first public railway in the world, they say, and the first gasworks, the first fireworks and the first fatal accident with a balloon. A Sydenham lad also scored the first goal on a Wednesday in Leap Year in the rain by a left-handed mid-field player named John . . . or something very similar. Most of these firsts either led to, or resulted from, the siting in Sydenham of the Victorian world's most exciting edifice—the Crystal Palace, whose name is now perpetuated as a sports centre.

People who live in the historic centre of town never give a second thought to such little pieces of time. They completely ignore the historic nature of the buildings in which they live. All too often they are too busy wangling planning permission to destroy them so they can exploit their land values and continue living in the consequently not-so-historic centre of town. But set a historic building down in a suburb and the suburb will never forget it. So it is with Sydenham, even though the building is no longer there. The Crystal Palace burned down, with or without encouragement, in 1936 and people have been talking about it ever since. They have been talking about arson, incompetence, bureaucracy, the splendid sight and the awful tragedy of the event. The holocaust overshadowed even the traffic accident. Sydenham people get a continuing frisson from such fatalities because these days life can be pretty flat on the high land which separates London from Kent.

On the face of it, you would not credit Sydenham people with much historical awareness. Where their buildings are not boarded up or falling down they are brand new. The extravagant Victorian architecture which went up at the same time as the Palace has given way to tiny hutches for today's truncated families. Sydenham was not developed in the 1930s along with most London suburbs. It was destroyed instead. What was begun in 1936 was finished in 1939. The war left post-war planners with a simple task—which did not include demolition. The German bombs cut through Sydenham with even less conscience than the flames engulfed the Crystal Palace, and what the bombs didn't destroy the defence forces did. They dismantled the old water towers of Isambard Kingdom Brunel so the enemy aircraft could not get them in their beam. After the war the eccentric old estates gave way to identical new estates, though not completely: Sydenham was as reluctant then as ever to acknowledge its passage into the twentieth century, to allow the demolition ball to sever the umbilical cord with its imperious past. Here and there some great white elephant of a mansion still lives out its dying years, hired out to film companies to make ends meet. It is due to this occasional continuing brush with celebrities that Sydenham people are slightly in awe of the show business world and several show business writers make their homes there. 'Katherine Hepburn has been to Sydenham!' they announce proudly, as the clichés pound off the typewriters to pay for their extravagant home improvements modelled on some soulless Californian suburban dream and completely out of place in the swirling mists of south London. Show business is a Sydenham tradition. 'Sarah Siddons once visited,' they whisper. 'And Jenny Lind, Gilbert *and* Sullivan, not to mention Dvořák, Mendelssohn, Rubinstein and, would you believe, Franz Liszt.' The Crystal Palace came to Sydenham they say, and not vice versa, for Sydenham was renowned for its music even before the building of the great glass house which resulted in vast concerts attended by the Emperor of Russia, the Shah of Persia and the Sultan of Zanzibar.

Music was, of course, the leisure activity of the Victorian nouveaux riches who moved into the area on the tracks of the Great Surrey Iron Railway and lit up their homes courtesy of the new-fangled Gas, Light and Coal Company. Sydenham people love to drop these evocative names, to claim historical connections which go back as far as Alfred the Great and to maintain that almost everybody you have ever heard of has been to Sydenham at one time or another, including a great many people who almost certainly have not. The list includes everybody anybody would ever like to meet: authors like Walter Scott, C.S. Forester, Nicholas Monsarrat, politicians like William Pitt and George Lansbury, explorers like Shackleton, the tea families Tetley and Horniman, the architect Barry who designed the Houses of Parliament. He also designed Dulwich College where Raymond Chandler went to school. And Lord Byron was briefly a pupil at another

Dulwich college. Those were the days before Sydenham achieved its monotonous, though locally highly prized, air of suburban respectability, its misbehaviour limited to the study of other people's idiosyncrasies. 'The Lord Mayor of London's mistress once lived here,' Sydenham people say. 'And the mistress of King William IV.' She did indeed. Mrs Allsop was the mother of ten of William's children and therefore a holder of another Sydenham record. With its fine air and fertile ground Sydenham was considered a great place for mistresses, its position just far enough removed from proper metropolitan society yet not so far removed as to suggest banishment to the bowels of the south-east, which today answers to the name of Croydon. Sydenham was rather élite in those days with its springs, wells and spas which were the equivalent of the modern sauna, sun-tan parlour and massage salon for the naughty, idle rich.

All that has changed. Just as Fulham people say they live in Chelsea and Earl's Court people say they live in the Royal Borough, everybody who lives anywhere near Sydenham these days automatically says they live in Dulwich. They like the serious air of scholarship Dulwich suggests. Residents of Anerley Park and Gipsy Hill, of Tulse Hill and Forest Hill, even those proud champions of the landmark that was the Crystal Palace, all say they live in Dulwich now. Today's Crystal Palace—with its caravan site, its fast food, its sports centre, its broadcasting aerial symbolic of the mass appropriation of every last secret by the people—is a much more plebeian reality than the crystal dream. Popes may visit it, as it was once visited by Royalty, only to be tarnished with the vulgarity which the twentieth century automatically bestows on its heroes by making them so available. Crystal Palace people wisely ignore the present and conjure up the past. They organise coach trips to Chatsworth to admire the surviving architecture of Joseph Paxton who built the Palace. 'Sir Joseph put Sydenham on the map,' they acknowledge. They attend lectures about his horticultural achievements, write booklets about their glorious history and encourage their children to make up poems about a heyday they never saw. They encourage them to focus totally on the remains of the Palace for their romance and their recreation, and organise nature rambles around its perimeter.

Sydenham has always had the reputation of believing in the virtues of a good education. For one thing a good education can help you to get out of Sydenham. These days its name only conjures up the natural amorphous indistinction it shares with all those similar adjacent suburbs: Beckenham, Wickham, Orpington, aptly described by their diminutive last syllables and synonymous only with middle-class anonymity and athletics. This is an area of modest bungalows, proper ambitions, well-tended sports grounds maintained by institutional employers eager to encourage the little imagination necessary to the arts of toeing the line, keeping in step and playing the game. Not only is it not distinguished by any exotica, it is not distinguished by any social facilities apart from the changing room. There is no lively shopping centre, no obvious gathering place, its pubs are old fashioned, the boutiques have not yet arrived. Modern culture has stopped on its lower slopes. Unlike Richmond Hill, which still continues to evoke the eighteenth century, Sydenham can genuinely only speak of it; unlike Muswell Hill, which has thrown itself into the twentieth century with its passion for useless artefacts hand-made in Taiwan and altered states of mind inherited from San Francisco, Sydenham is still looking for its future. That is why Sydenham people so avidly champion the possibilities. Why they talk endlessly of the potential of the low-level station and the high-level site and try to forge cultural

links with Alexandra Palace people by encouraging them
to share their regrets at the recent similar demise by fire of
their own Palace.

North London people only warily watch all this south
London solidarity. If they envy them their history they do
not envy them their uniformity. They do not envy them
their landscaped lawns, their electric mowers or their
clapboard housing estates, which lend Sydenham the
appearance in parts of a custom-built North American
suburb. Canadian officials head straight for Sydenham
when faced with a spell in this country, and it is not
difficult to see why. Its tree-lined roads and wooden
architecture have their parallel in any modern suburb of
Toronto. The naïve conveniences of its high street include
the sort of hamburger with liquor joint that Americans
equate with a sophisticated night out. It is all too straight-
forward to be inspired. H. G. Wells who once loitered in
Sydenham's woods, Van Gogh who liked its atmospheric
view, would hardly embark on the tortures of the South
Circular Road to make an emotional pilgrimage to Sydenham today. The clapboard, the traditional method of
building in Kent, is all that is really left of history. That is
why, like the North Americans who feel that they too have
too feeble a grip on the past, Sydenham people are
constantly trying to evoke it.

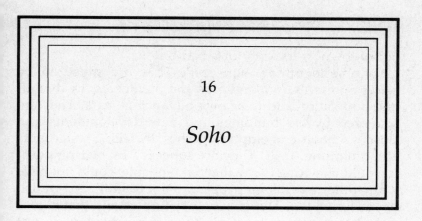

16

Soho

WAY BACK IN the 'Sixties I answered a small ad in the evening paper for a pied-à-terre in Soho: 3 rooms k & b, £8 per week. Those were the days when you could have an evening at the cinema, a steak dinner for two, a packet of fags and a cab home and still have change from half-a-crown. This flat was quite something, wall to wall carpeting and a private roof garden overlooking the porno cinema in the street below. It was definitely designed for something other than chucking cherry stones down off the flat roof onto passers-by in a fit of euphoric youth, now I come to think of it. My landlord certainly thought so. He was about seven foot cubed, an Antipodean wrestling champion who practised on his girlfriends every night in the first-floor flat. When he had complaints about the cherry stones, he stormed upstairs looking every cubic inch like King Kong. Fay Wray, I melted before his clenched frown. 'You are the only "nice" girl in my empire,' he breathed from every bicep. 'If you do things like that I might as well multiply the rent by ten and put in the vice.' Today the flat is still rented to a nice girl for three times the price I paid, and the rates add half as much again. For that you get a lot of black rubbish bags in the porch, a lot of pits in the street, tramps in the alleys and out-of-towners looking for a bad time.

Soho residents are squeezed. They are squeezed by prices and vices and landlords and bulldozers, by dwindling population and their own advancing years. They are squeezed by old buildings and new developments and closing schools and empty churches, by failing restaurants and mounting trash. They are squeezed by blazing porn. It would be wrong to say that Soho people would not have it any other way. Soho people are not bashful, or prudish or small-minded. This is why they understand that it does not always pay to let it all hang out, that you do not necessarily get twice the fun for twice the display, and you do not necessarily get twice the money either. Soho people understand the layers of life, that people are as good as they are bad, that a quick buck turned is not necessarily despicable, and neither, necessarily, is the manner in which you turn it. It all depends. Soho people can be right where Mrs Whitehouse can be wrong. More than that, they can both be right together. The overt quashing of overt vice is more antipathetic to the quality of life than the existence of discreet sins side by side with discreet virtues. Soho people are not flirtatious and they do not invite trouble. They are survivors who aim to enjoy getting by, and by these qualities alone are they recognised.

Soho has only three thousand residents. Twenty years ago it had six thousand, two generations ago thirty thousand. As with much of the centre of London, the real vitality of day-to-day life in Soho is forever threatened by bureaucracy on the one hand and high rollers on the other. It has been decreed that central areas should be a total commercial enterprise whether or not this is to anyone's ultimate advantage. People who want to live and raise families in central London today have to move mountains and the local council to keep things moving sluggishly their way. The effort makes them doubly committed. They turn a blind eye to the disadvantages and try to look forward to a time when their sticking power will be rewarded by the usual cyclical change in any one area's circumstances.

Many people who do not actually live in Soho think of themselves as Soho people. Soho has an entire proxy population, quite apart from its tourists. Jazz fans and journalists, raconteurs and bon viveurs, gamblers, dissidents, part-time hookers, addicts of pastis and pinball and pasta, of monosodium glutamate and of Continental cuts, painters, poseurs and pavement artists. Proxy Soho people think of themselves as avant-garde, but they are actually seeking to summon back the days when Soho was London's Hampstead, Knightsbridge and Chelsea all in one. That was nearly three hundred years ago. In those days the word 'soho' was a hunting cry like tallyho; now it is still a hunting cry, though less in the hedgerow than the bordello. Those Soho hangers-on who are too sophisticated for this sort of thing go there because Blake was born there and had his visions, because De Quincey lived there with his opium eater. Because Mozart, Constable and Hazlitt worked there; because Charles II kept Nell Gwyn in Meard Street and the costly courtesan Mrs Cornelys lived in Soho Square. Casanova, who was a frequent visitor to her salon, would never expect to find anyone as fashionable as Mrs Cornelys today in the same business in Soho Square. Two churches share it with a hospital, half the film business and a house for women, fallen not so much from grace, but on hard times. Proxy Soho people are often ignorant about the present. They go there because revolutions were plotted there in the past, and scientific breakthroughs were made there. Because Karl Marx wrote *Das Kapital* in the Quo Vadis, unhampered by singing waiters, the first television pictures were transmitted from upstairs in Bianchi's by John Logie Baird, and because a Dr Snow pinpointed cholera outside Ron McCrindle's pub. Soho has always been synonymous with invention, and nowadays they have to invent ways of making a peep-show interesting. People who go for business lunches in L'Epicure and L'Escargot may not appreciate this as they run the gauntlet of neon signs advertising strip, porn, sleaze and tease on their way to a serious tête-à-tête about the future of Society.

Soho hangers-on believe their attachment to the area is about art, not commerce. They would never openly enter Raymond's Revue Bar with a Japanese motor car salesman and a Wigan rugby fan. They swear they have never sampled the delights of Cayenne Pepper or Suzie Wong. They go there for nourishment of another kind. They take their elevenses at the Swiss, insult each other at the Coach and Horses, eat lunch at the Gay Hussar (if someone else is paying), carry on drinking at the Colony, have tea at Valerie's, their last rounds in the French, a nightcap in Ronnie Scott's and take a taxi home. Since most of them are media men, or would like to be when they are upright, this aspect of Soho gets far too much publicity.

If all the proxy Soho people moved into Soho, Soho would be voyeuristic. Proxy Soho people get a frisson from brushing shoulders with the vice though they may pay lip-service to the idea of virtue; real Soho people brush shoulders daily with the vice and try to see some virtue in it. Soho people do not deplore the strip shows and the ladies who may or may not come from gay Paree. They don't mind what goes on behind darkened doors. They never ask questions because, no matter what the real answer to them might be, Soho people have a perfectly good one of their own. Soho people call exotic ladies with Yorkshire terriers 'mannequins'. Mannequins are beautiful to look at and give generously to the local kids at

Christmas because God has failed to provide them with their own families. Old mannequins become personal maids to new mannequins. These are proper supportive traditions with which Soho people feel safe. Soho people do not deplore models with bell-pushes who provide a necessary service to mankind. They do, however, deplore sleaze on the streets. They do not dislike peep-shows, but they are against neon signs. They do not like to be embarrassed by such things because it takes other business away. Soho barrow boys cannot get a good price for their bananas if their customers become too red-faced along the way. Soho people keep quiet about human frailty. They walk the long way round the vice and have the Marquee sound-proofed.

Soho people wilt in the suburbs, even though it is the express wish of certain interfering figureheads to transplant them for their own good. It is not good for them. Soho people are more alarmed by rows of standard roses than by rows of eccentric winos; more depressed by acres of clipped lawns than by claustrophobic concrete courtyards; more afraid of airy modern houses than of dank Victorian slums. This has been proved again and again. Relocated Soho mothers feel trapped by the clean smells of new plasterwork and futuristic plumbing. They stand helplessly in the middle of empty rooms and wish themselves wholeheartedly back in the tenement buildings. This is because they are either Chinese, Bengali or Italian. Sometimes they are still Jewish and French. Their fathers came from intimate southern cities, their mothers from crowded northern ghettoes. They dance to archaic tunes and have faith in primitive traditions. They know each other by first names and by nicknames. They know each other's failures and triumphs, illnesses and deaths. The blame is ascribed not to individuals, but to life. They know each other's children and they watch out for them in

the streets. They are tailors and shopkeepers, waiters and
cooks. They understand service as well as self and have
few prejudices because they can't afford them. Catholic
and Jew meet at Christian socials.

They send their children to Italian lessons to keep in
touch with their kind, to Hebrew lessons and to Chinese.
They also send them to English school. Soho people are
very ambitious for their children and their children tend to
reward their ambition. They are not the teenagers who
hang round the basement clubs with their hair dyed
purple, sniffing glue when they are not spraying it on
their coxcombs. These are not the young people who get
hooked on Chinese heroin or break into tourist cars or
hang round Piccadilly waiting for their next injection of
legalised methadone. These children don't even eat in the
restaurants where their parents work, or drink in the
pubs. Soho children are at home eating motzahs like
mother makes and studying to be nurses, lawyers and
economists. They go to youth clubs and church socials
with their parents. Because they have been brought up so
correctly they do not expect to live in Soho as it is now
when they grow up. Soho children will marry other nice
children and move meekly to the suburbs, leaving Soho to
other people who need or crave or are resigned to a raw
struggle in life. Reality is their only security and their
luxury is their licence to be themselves. Suburban people
call this dangerously eccentric. Soho people call it worldly,
and if you can't see it they are not about to spell it out.

You might not think, to visit Robin Moon in the small
flat he has occupied along with a whole aviary of free-
flying birds for the last sixty years, that he is master chef to
Christina Foyle and the Royal Geographical Society. You
might not think, to visit seventy-eight-year-old Frankie
Blake, wrestling champion, in his third floor walk-up
behind a strip joint, that his brother is a senior Jesuit priest

in Mayfair. You might think, as one bank manager did, with letting space above his business premises, to floor a prospective female tenant in the world's oldest profession by asking for impeccable references.

'Like who?' she asked.

'Like an archbishop and at least two MPs,' the bank manager insisted.

'No problem,' said she. And it wasn't.

Soho people keep a low profile. They entertain their friends and indulge their hobbies behind impersonal façades, and during the week the passing commuter scarcely suspects they are there. On Sunday mornings they step out in their dressing gowns to buy the newspapers. They buy goat's milk at their own dairy and homemade bread from their own bakers. They chat on the corner of the streets. That's when you know for sure that Soho is a village. Councillors, who want to raze the eighteenth-century houses and replace them with little boxes, can never turn it into the suburbs. Soho exists because of the suburbs. Councillors who fail to press for legislation against facilitating leases to porno merchants are being cynical about their own environment. Soho people are not cynical themselves but they have no pat answers with which to manipulate the flow of life. They are not sophisticated enough to imagine there are any. They do not want to make cuckoo clocks in the age of quartz movements, they can merely hope individually that they will not be mown down before their time. Some hope, they sometimes fear—for each one knows how his family came there from other ghettoes in the first place.

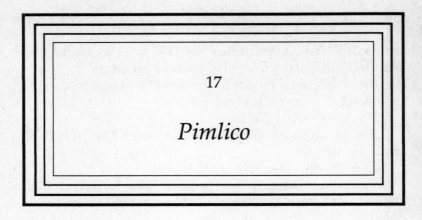

17

Pimlico

ALL OVER LONDON—and everywhere else in the world too for that matter—everybody, no matter who they are, distinguishes themselves in their daily mundane round by the simplest of recurring decisions: what to eat, wear, drive, hang on their walls and plant in their gardens. According to these decisions they know exactly where to make their homes. There are no accidents about this, only inevitabilities which are as transparent to the onlooker as they are apparently mysterious to their ritual exponents.

There is one exception to this rule—Pimlico. Pimlico is a mystery to absolutely everyone: a sprawling, incoherent conglomeration of people of all classes, ages, nationalities, colours, ambitions and passing fancies, who nonetheless have in common the fact that they enjoy being a (tangential) part of a sprawling, incoherent conglomeration of people of all classes, nationalities, ages, colours, ambitions and passing fancies. This is often because they are doing something unacceptable on the more rigid tracks of society and they don't necessarily want anyone else to easily zero in on it. Earl's Court and Notting Hill people vaunt their peculiarities. Not so Pimlico people. This does not mean that they have none. Pimlico people are contrary. If they are landed they are trying to prove otherwise, if they are landless they are snuggling up to the seats of power. If they are married they are living in sin, if they are widowed they are too merry, if they are gay they are passing for straight, if they are living on the dole they are exaggerating their circumstances. If they are elderly they are still anarchistic, if they are young they are premature schemers.

People who live in Putney, Richmond and Kew report each other to their neighbours for any one of these misdemeanours. Nobody ever reports anyone in Pimlico because they neither know whom to report nor whom to report them to. They do not know who is their nextdoor neighbour and they do not care to find out because they do not want to be landed with the responsibility. They do not know whether their private hotels are full of commercial travellers or spies, whether their boarding houses shelter trippers or tarts. Old men with baby brides, youngsters with ageing floosies, actresses high on indiscretions, writers high on observations, politicians loose in love-nests, lone theoreticians, marriage partners living with other people's marriage partners, marriage partners living with their own unsuitable marriage partners, mixed liaisons, black with white, rich with poor, the kind and the cruel, gamblers and puritans—in short, all sorts of ill-assorted pairs who would never be acceptable in St John's Wood or Clapham get off scot-free without so much as a raised eyebrow in Pimlico.

Pimlico people do not like to be pinned down and they defy you to try it. Pimlico is not bijou like Chelsea, nor grand like Belgravia, nor powerful like Westminster, nor shifting like Victoria, nor depressed like Vauxhall, all of which are its immediate neighbours. It is some of all of these things. It is vicarious and anonymous, lonesome yet playing at being a part of the establishment. Pimlico people do not flash their money, they do not sigh about

art, they do not dissect literature or politics, or boast of the
fineness of their cellars or their cuisine. They do not refer
to these things because they are not as familiar with them
as they would like to be. They envy the past and look
forward to a future where its happier achievements will be
available to Pimlico people. Meanwhile they are waiting in
the wings. They do not press you with invitations nor
compete with your successes. They do not think they are
either mean or philistine. They are secretive about their
ambitions, egalitarian in their outward behaviour, secure
in the knowledge that they must be special, tasteful, well-
connected and clever to have found a piece of reasonably
priced real estate right at the hub of urban desirability.

Pimlico is bounded and gridded by some agreeable
symbols of power. On its perimeters are the River
Thames, the Tate Gallery, the Palace, and Dolphin Square,
the model apartment block which stands on the site of
what was a model factory. Its streets are called discreetly
for the more intimate first names of the Grosvenor family
who own them: Hugh, for instance, and Lupus. Its shops
are shopped in by old retainers and by Filipino maids. Its
supermarkets stand cheek by jowl with those quaint
personal businesses which vanished from other parts of
London more than twenty years ago. Its model housing
estates are black, its architectural showpiece, within
shrieking distance of the bourgeois eardrums of Dolphin
Square, is a comprehensive school which looks like a
greenhouse and does its best to turn out flower children.

Pimlico people benefit a good deal from these contradictions. Contradictions keep prices down. Pimlico people
are more thrifty than stuffy, more street-smart than
snobbish. Pimlico could be as elegant as Belgravia, whose
architecture it shares and on whose borders it falters; it
could be as barren as Nine Elms. Its whitewashed façades
are a disgrace compared to those on its northern bound-

ary, its council estates brilliant compared to those on its southern one. Pimlico people, whether from the housing estate or the Grosvenor Estate, do not complain. Their markets are full of delicacies for the aristocracy at council house prices. Fancy a plucked quail, a jugged hare, some fresh lychees or gulls' eggs? Go to Pimlico. Go there if your taste buds blossom at the thought of a kilo of crab or crisp *crevettes grises*. But do not eat them there unless you want to sit portentously among the die-hard Dolphin Square brigadiers with their dyed divorcées, or the overflow from St John's Wood at the White Elephant on the river. Most other Pimlico restaurants are like Notting Hill restaurants: long on pretensions and short on expertise, full of young men in floor-length striped aprons peddling mother's home recipes to other hoorays whose palates got blunted in some country nursery. In Pimlico you may encounter any number of utility pies.

This is all the same to Pimlico visitors who expect such legendary things of English cooking, and of whom there are very many, freshly decanted each day from the Continental boat-trains at Victoria Station. Americans seek better pastures than Pimlico and Arabs are not much at home here, but Germans, Greeks and Belgians pile from the second-class carriages into the peeling Pimlico hotels. Especially Belgians. Belgians love Pimlico and keep coming back for generations, possibly because it is a good deal more exciting than downtown Brussels on a Saturday night in any season, even now that it is full of randy Euro-MPs.

Belgians also like the beer. Pimlico beer has been famous for three centuries, and there is not much else Pimlico has been famous for. Infamous is something else. Time was when the district was nothing but a nauseating marsh stretching between Buckingham Palace and the river. In those days the Palace was called Arlington

House. It had a clear view of the water to the south and the west, interrupted only by the chimney of the brewery and the odd peasant plucking at the osier beds. The peasants universally succumbed to something known as the 'staggers', which is the sort of name favoured these days by amateur Pimlico restaurateurs. It is one of the mysteries of history as to whether the 'staggers' refers to the effect of the food, the beer or the gases from the marshes.

The very name Pimlico is a mystery, particularly since it has its origins not in Pimlico at all but in Hoxton, right the other side of town. This is a parish which has very little in common with Pimlico today, where one publican of Italian descent is supposed to have kept a rowdy house where a good time could be had by one and all. His name is perpetuated in Hoxton these days by a certain Pimlico Walk. Pimlico proper is synonymous with the good time which used to be available in Hoxton. At Jenny's Whim, the pleasure gardens by the river, all sorts of lords and ladies from elsewhere in town dallied with all sorts of local riff-raff. The big house was called Tart House. Pimlico was spelt Pimplico in the parish registers—why? No one knows; both derivations have been discreetly lost in the mists emanating from the infamous marshes.

Pimlico has been trying to improve its image ever since—without becoming boringly respectable, you understand. Just as it made some outward progress it was flattened by those German bombs which narrowly missed Victoria Station during the Second World War, which is one reason for its current architectural schizophrenia. These days decaying house hulks are being converted into charming little bachelor flats which in nearby Chelsea would be labelled *pied-à-terres*. Because Pimlico is so near to Chelsea they are full of *bric-à-brac*, *pot pourri*, *jalousies* and *jardinières*. The nearer Pimlico gets to Chelsea the more it loses its own identity. Here prices rocket, not to mention pretensions, and the focal points of border-dwellers become more and more fixed. But Pimlico proper is essentially mobile. It is bisected, traversed, ringed and crossed by railway tracks and arterial roads. Trains rumble through it above and below ground, lorries hum towards the South Circular, commuters tailgate on the Embankment, taxis cruise the hotels. Many people pass through Pimlico daily without even noticing they have been there, without even knowing where it is.

All this pleases proper Pimlico people. People who have tried to live in Hampstead or Chelsea, and hated those places because of their pretensions, love Pimlico because they imagine it has none. People who have been ousted from Bayswater by arriviste property sharks derive some false sense of comfort from the family trees of their own landlords. Loners who have been squeezed out of Soho by the overt vice of the place or out of Mayfair by the unrewarding prices, pounce on Pimlico. Pimlico people have something in common with Soho people and Mayfair people. They like the gutter life behind the powerful façades. They need the thrills these things inspire, but this is no easy combination of thrills to find. No matter how much milling there is in Clapham, Pimlico people would die in Clapham of withdrawal symptoms from the corridors of power. No matter how much power is concentrated in Belgravia Pimlico people feel safer on the wrong side of Ebury Street. They can potter in Pimlico because they are poorer. They can be less responsible in Pimlico. They can be less identifiable. Life in Islington would be anathema to Pimlico people because Islington people are such aggressive and self-conscious students of their own identity. Islington people move as a group with group consciousness. They have meaningful affairs, cross references and homespun philosophies. They are intellectual snobs with a block culture and a diary open to the world. They are the exact opposite of Pimlico people. Regular snobs who like to pass others as ships in the night move to Pimlico. Pimlico is anonymous. You need no passport to get into it. Pimlico is No Man's Land. And from No Man's Land you can move in any direction.

18

Notting Hill

THE SAYING GOES that if you tilted the United States on its side, all the odds and ends would finish up in California. If you tilted London on its side all the odds and ends would finish up in Notting Hill.

Notting Hill is an extremely seductive part of London, although its wide avenues and high façades boast mostly faded glory. Those who can afford to do so, do up their homes; those who cannot, board them up. This may happen in the same street—or even in the same building—which is why Notting Hill is not a safe place for those solely interested in investment. Notting Hill has never gone all the way down, but neither has it come all the way up. Sociologists, teachers and students of life marvel at the colourful fluidity of the neighbourhood. Art students live off it. Yet few people other than Rachman have dared to become heavily involved as landlords. Brave pioneers have bought houses in it and then fled its vicissitudes.

Notting Hill is unpredictable. Creeping graffiti take over the peeling whitewash and Victorian slums make way for council ones. Grand colonial mansions co-exist with corrugated iron, white liberals with black liberals. Notting Hill is very liberal indeed. Notting Hill is liberal to the point of lunacy. If pottery is the major art form in Fulham and placemats the major art form in Richmond, lunacy is the art indigenous to Notting Hill. There is no one form of lunacy in the area—indeed that is the whole point of lunacy. There may be as many forms of lunacy as there are people. The main thing is to be out on a limb, but if everyone is out on the same limb this is known as suburban. If everyone is out on a different limb, this is known as Notting Hill.

Notting Hill people would be very uncomfortable in the suburbs, just as suburban people would be very uncomfortable in Notting Hill. The suburbs do not openly encourage green hair and glue-sniffing, art movies and dissident rock. They take exception to fringe politics, tricky intellectuals, witchcraft, vandalism and fun. They do not like to see people in fancy dress in broad daylight, hanging out on street corners in all weathers, eating malodorous takeaway foreign food, wearing more hair than clothes and bopping to a few thousand decibels to which the rest of the neighbourhood is forced to listen. Suburbanites are not keen on mixed marriages and second-hand wardrobes, too much make-up and too few undergarments. They do not like to see purple worn with pink nor red worn with orange. They don't care for art on the walls (never mind on the streets) but prefer it safely tucked away in safely supervised galleries. They do not like to see droves of nymphets in tennis shoes unless they are on the way to the local tennis club. Slim chance in Notting Hill.

Such things make suburban people nervous. They like to be able to leave their two-year-old cars outside their houses without their neighbours scratching things like EAT THE RICH into the paintwork on the bonnet. They like to be able to walk through the streets without being bottled by yobbos, mugged by minors and robbed by anyone who stops to ask them the time. They like to be able to drop into the local for a pick-me-up without someone breaking down the bar around them. Notting Hill people take a risk on this sort of thing every time they leave the house. Some Notting Hill people don't even have to leave the house to live dangerously. They do not necessarily expect to see the fathers of their children ever again, or, for that matter, the children themselves. They do not expect to see their cars in the morning if they leave them on the streets at night. They dare not for a moment let go of a dog or a bike or a pram, or flaunt a shopping basket or a pound note. Every year there are more than five thousand burglaries, deceptions, assaults and thefts in Notting Hill. Every year there are nearly three thousand cases of petty damage and bicycle theft. More than two thousand cars disappear, or their contents. Notting Hill creditors settle matters with broken arms and busted noses. Notting Hill police burst in first and ask questions later. So popular are assaults on other people in this part of the world that one pub is universally nicknamed the GBH.

When Notting Hill people are not in the GBH looking forward to a knee-capping, they are scoring some other sort of dubious activity in another pub, where middle-aged, unnatural blondes hang out with black eyes and black escorts. When they are not drinking rum and Red Stripe these people are likely to appear as bit-part actors in television about real life like *The Sweeney*. Notting Hill is where life and art meet and neither triumphs. That is why Notting Hill people live there. But, unlike Earl's Court—where things are so unsavoury that people boast that they live in the Royal Borough of Kensington and Chelsea—Notting Hill people never disown Notting Hill or rename it deceptively. They are proud of the Gate, as they call it, as in gate-crash, gate-money, gate-fold and Newgate.

People who live in much grander adjacent places, in Holland Park, in Campden Hill, in Bayswater, are all apt to say that they live in Notting Hill. People who live in Belgravia are apt to visit it to pursue at least some of their vices. Instability and possibility is the whole point of living in the area and addiction or predilection to thrills or even spills. Few people, after all, move away from Los Angeles just because they know they can get shot going out to dinner. Notting Hill people are a lot like Los Angeles people. They are fringe people first and foremost, crazy for all the fads they fancy. They enjoy brinkmanship and they enjoy provocation. They are not rich and it is not entirely certain whether they would really like to be, even if they do make the odd attempt at someone else's expense. They live by their wits, by their eccentricities and by their unpredictabilities.

Whereas Hampstead thinkers always agree with other Hampstead thinkers, Notting Hill thinkers do not even agree with what they themselves thought yesterday. Notting Hill is open to new ideas. Notting Hill is a market-place, and not just on Saturday down the Portobello Road. What you can see is for tourists: the locals buy what you can't. Notting Hill markets the most meagre talent. If you are a drag queen you have no intention of becoming Danny La Rue. If you are a housewife you recycle what you have in your closet—possibly to a drag queen. Closet knitters open stalls of baby clothes. Landladies boil down slivers of soiled soap and sell them as marbled toiletries. Amateur gardeners open 'head' shops, amateur cooks sell cups of lentil soup. Yesterday's ethnic frocks become tomorrow's fashion points.

Notting Hill people are much more avant-garde than Chelsea people think they are. Chelsea people never know what to buy until Notting Hill has given up buying it long ago. By the time fashions reach Chelsea they have been cleaned up, toned down and packaged ready for the consumer classes. Notting Hill people are meanwhile already on to something else. If Notting Hill discovers Victorian water closets, Chelsea people will discover them two years later. Two years after that they will be heralded in Camden Passage. Five years on Clapham will be delighted by them, and Clapham people will be faking them. Ten years on Sotheby's will charge the earth and the fake will be part of history.

Notting Hill discovered the Pill, hippies, the 'Sixties, communes and squatting. Notting Hill discovered cruising when Earl's Court was full of brigadiers. Many of the gays in Notting Hill make most of the gays in Earl's Court look like amateur theatricals. Notting Hill gays would never wear anything as butch as leather. They go about their business wearing 'his and his' sweaters and matching 'taches'. Notting Hill was first with reggae, first with punk and first with New Wave. Hampstead people still think New Wave refers to a French film made in the 'Fifties. Notting Hill people know that New Wave is already Old Hat. They have forgotten all about the 'Fifties, they have forgotten all about the 'Sixties, and the 'Seventies, and they don't have much time for the 'Eighties. Notting Hill people, like Los Angeles people, are living in another century and they are not sure whether it is all coming or whether it has been.

People who suspect Los Angeles people of peculiar and unnatural behaviour say they are shallow, vain and loony because of the sun. 'Off the wall', they say, 'Out to lunch', or, 'Their brains are fried'. There is very little sun in Notting Hill, but this does not stop them behaving as if it were situated right on top of the equator. This is because many Notting Hill people come from sunny climes. Old habits die hard. Whereas Pakistanis come to these shores and immediately find a niche for themselves in the

bureaucracy, West Indians come here and carry on behaving exactly as if they were in the West Indies. They don't
seem to notice the weather. Where once they boogied on
the beaches now they boogie in the streets. They boogie in
the shops and down the dole and up the Mangrove, if the
police don't get there first, and if they do they boogie just
wherever they happen to find themselves. If they can take
along a steel band, so much the better and if they can take
along two, better still. Two steel bands is a carnival. If no
steel bands are available, they take along a transistor radio
with stereo speakers and shoulder straps or a Sony
Walkman with the latest cassette, and they boogie along
on roller-skates in the gutter with wings fitted to their
ankles. Notting Hill was first with roller-skating. While
other Londoners are painfully jogging, Notting Hill
people are painlessly doing it on wheels.

People who do not live in Notting Hill are apt to assume
that all these colourful pyrotechnics accompanied by
blatant decibels must constitute some sort of menace, if
not to the peace of the community at least to their own
peace of mind. These people can be seen cowering at the
Carnival thinking how jolly quaint this alien culture is
once a year. This is a point of view promoted by the
media, who like nothing better than to feature some jolly
English cop hand in hand with some Jamaican Momma
suggesting not only that there is something unusual about
friendly race relations in London but that the authorities
are well to the forefront in promoting them. This is a false
picture. The Notting Hill Carnival is not a truce between
white and black in Notting Hill, but a truce between a
society and its authorities—and a very contrived one at
that—which is as liable to explosion as any other piece of
fiction. There are no bad race relations in London that are
half as bad as fear of them by insecure young people in the
secure uniform of office. Notting Hill people of all hues are

provocative, and they are never more provocative than when they are expected to be.

Simply hanging out (which is a Mediterranean and American tradition inspired by the superior climate in those places) is rarely provocative to anyone else but the English, who are apt to consider that the nicest things done in public are open to suspicion while the most grotesque things done in private are okay. Doubtless there are many grotesque things done in private in Notting Hill, and not only by people who don't know any better. The 'nice' fringes of the area are full of painters, writers, historians, politicians and socialites with more family background than future ambition. These Notting Hill literati are unusual among the locals in that they are at least literate, though that does not mean they are necessarily published. A piece of graffiti on the telephone box wall is probably read by more people than a Notting Hill poem, which is usually read aloud in some rat-infested basement to a handful of rats by the poet himself accompanied by a sitar and a sandalwood joss stick. Most Notting Hill people do not write, they simply use the phone, if it has not been vandalised. They like their transactions to be transitory and to go unrecorded, and even those which are done on street corners are done so not to provoke interest, but to offer a degree of anonymity to the parties which does not come from trading at a fixed address.

The moral of all this is that white people in Notting Hill like most of the things black people do, including their rice and their vices. They try to boogie too and wear their hair in beaded plaits. They wear Rastafarian woolly caps and when they are not sniffing glue, they put it on their hair to make it stand on end. The head is all important in Notting Hill—what is on it, what is in it and what is not. Notting Hill people like nothing better than that light-headed feeling. They grow Portobello Gold in their window boxes, sniff angel dust, drop acid or simply starve themselves into taking off. Notting Hill people can get very excited over a nice nut cutlet or a sliver of tasteless Chinese radish. Some of the unhealthiest-looking people in London can be found queueing up to buy health food in Notting Hill. This leaves them pasty and undernourished but in touch with more spiritual things. Spirituality is extremely popular in this part of town. There is nowhere more full of religious sects of all sorts, unless, of course, it is Los Angeles. Synagogues rub shoulders with Baptist chapels, Arab Christians with Holy Rollers and Jehovah's Witnesses. Spot a blue building in Notting Hill and it is more than likely to be a place where someone or other goes to worship. Everything else is painted in icecream colours, which is also true of Los Angeles. Those people in both places who are not born-again Christians are likely to be gurus and witches.

Notting Hill people are superstitious because they are pinning their faith on the hope that something will turn up, and existing meanwhile more or less on charity. When it does, and they can afford it, they get on a 747 and finally move to Los Angeles for real. When they come back to London they move to Kensington or to Belgravia and never stray nearer the fly-over than the Portobello Hotel. But all their lives they fondly turn over in their minds their happy if inaccurate memories of a typically inspiring set-up in the early history of Notting Hill: Alice B. Toklas, Che Guevara and Cecil Beaton all sharing a basement bedsitter before they rudely encountered real life.

19

Fulham

PEOPLE WHO DO not live in Fulham are always encouraging other people to do so, even though they would never dream of living there themselves. This includes ex-husbands and aristocratic parents who have not yet fallen on hard times and do not intend doing so because of any misplaced responsibilities towards their ex-wives or their young. This is where Fulham comes in. 'Fulham is so handy,' they say to the person who is about to live there. 'So convenient for town.' 'It's such a good investment,' they say to themselves. 'We can't go wrong. Fulham has amenities. What a marvellous place to bring up children! Why, Fulham has schools, social services, doctors, some of the few remaining hospitals in London. It has a huge cemetery.' Fulham is a pretty good place to live—and die.

Fulham is the divorcées' graveyard. Knock on any Fulham door and you are liable to come face to face with some faintly recognisable female you once met over a dining table in happier circumstances somewhere a couple of miles to the East. Husbands all over Mayfair, Kensington, Belgravia and Chelsea always think of Fulham when they are about to off-load their wives. Naturally they never point out that Fulham is dour, dirty, grey and cramped.

They never point out that it is extremely ugly, unless you live in Hurlingham, Parsons Green or Stamford Bridge, where the houses are far too overpriced to be second homes. This does not necessarily mean that they are architectural gems. Still, Fulham people always say they live in Hurlingham, Parsons Green or Stamford Bridge when asked—if not right in the heart of Chelsea. When pressed in the interests of total accuracy, they say they have a little house *just off* Parsons Green, or *round the corner* from the Hurlingham Club, or *at the bend* of the King's Road. When discovered they explain that Fulham is not as pretentious as its neighbour Chelsea, nor as suburban as its neighbour Putney. They stress that it has a market, a river, a green and a palace, making it sound for all the world as rustic as Richmond-on-Thames.

In point of fact, Fulham is an amorphous mass of exactly identical streets lined with exactly identical houses, face-lifted with exactly identical paint jobs in cobalt blue, mustard yellow, pistaccio green or hot terra cotta pointed with white. No matter how bright the paint jobs, however, there is a leaden look about these houses, a pinched and peering quality to their terraces, as though as tiny saplings they had been planted too close together and had grown up etiolated and manic, searching for the sky. The streets in which they find themselves are either dismally bare or overcast with trees which are cut back in winter to resemble leprous amputees. In summer they suddenly burgeon to block out all light. This ensures that Fulham is as depressing in summer as in winter. Under the trees are rows of tightly packed cars with long-forgotten punctures, covered either in tarpaulins or in the leaves of these trees with their sticky secretions. In Fulham it is apparently not necessary to renovate these cars. Fulham people leave them where they are and go by train. Fulham has three handy underground stations. Fulham cannot make up its mind whether it is very, very handy or absolutely horrid, whether it is consciously up-and-coming or complacently down-and-out.

Unlike Clapham, where people vaunt its gentrification and stick brass knockers on all their stripped pine doors, Fulham people have a strange compulsion to degentrify. They go to Fulham because they believe in demystification, classlessness and uniformity, no matter how well-born they are. They go to Fulham because they will be in good company while not having to try so hard. They go to Fulham because they have scandalous pasts and inscrutable futures. Fulham people like to cut other people down to size because invariably they have taken a nasty knock themselves somewhere along the way. They like it because it is egalitarian but not yet totally beyond the pale, for most important of all it is north of the River. All this means that nothing will adversely affect Fulham real estate. Fulham people know that other people know that anything sandwiched between swinging Chelsea and proper Putney cannot be all bad. Ex-husbands know that it is easy to drop in and pick up the children on their way to their weekend houses in Berkshire, Wiltshire and Hampshire. Maybe they *do* pick up the children from time to time, but they never drop in unless they can possibly help it because they can be pretty sure they will find sticky fingerprints all over the decorator wallpaper, coffee stains on the cushions, bicycles in the dining room, dirty dishes in the bed and tortoises in the bath. Fulham children are allowed to run riot as a reaction to the stuffiness of their mothers' previous lives. They are allowed to scratch their names on the veneer of the television set, to grow penicillin in their tooth mugs, to sleep with the dog and eat with the cat. This is known as 'self-expression'. No one minds how Fulham children express themselves. Fulham children go to state schools and jolly well like it. If they complain about anything, or if anyone complains about them, their absentee fathers are to blame.

All this is designed to keep male chauvinism at bay. It is designed to keep establishment chauvinism at bay. Having lost out on the great social competition which is marriage, Fulham wives want to be loved for themselves, not for their achievements. They reserve the right to rise at midday, and wear dressing gowns at teatime whoever is coming to tea. To bite their fingernails and look a mess in public as well as private if they want to. To have hysterics where and when, never to open a book nor wear an oven glove or a cocktail frock. Not to be intellectual, feminine or enterprising. In short, to do nothing except just be. This means that Fulham women are far more liberated than Hampstead women who hope to goodness they are liberated and are always trying to prove it by writing another volume about menstruation or Jane Austen, or menstruation in Jane Austen. They are much more liberated than Richmond women who are always on the point of popping a Marks & Spencer's frozen pizza in the oven or feeding the pot plants. They are much, much more liberated than Clapham women who are always desperately dreaming up some new advertising jingle while juggling with a dinner party for ten.

Fulham women enjoy resting. Whether they ever wanted to be television actresses or researchers, designers of children's clothes or photographers' assistants, infant school teachers, mistresses or models, once in Fulham they throw themselves into living in Fulham.

They degenerate into squalor. They cultivate a certain downward mobility. Unlike Islington people who seek to proselytise among the working classes, Fulham people seek to blend with them.

In fact they do not blend at all. The working classes have far too much pride in appearances. They would never paint their living rooms purple and collect empty rusty tins of old-fashioned working-class products. They like their tea in teabags, not in Edwardian Typhoo tins. They still believe in washing their dishes, putting out their rubbish and they still expect their children to do well at school. Nouveau Fulham people find all this far too much like the inhibiting life they left behind. They want some room to drink herbal tea, to throw the I Ching, watch the cockroaches multiply, read magazines on astrology and have lots of affairs at the same time with people of either sex so they can never be tempted to put their faith in any one of them. Fulham people like to discuss among themselves the more meaningful aspects of socialism— like how to get more from the dole and where to enrol for subsidised pottery classes. These allow you to take home your own ashtray for use with your roll-your-own cigarettes. Pottery is a major art form in Fulham along with macramé matting and paper blinds (hand painted). It is aesthetic and useful but not professional. Fulham people read the *Guardian* because of its printing errors. They deplore perfection and enjoy rough-edged idiosyncrasy, rather like Marie-Antoinette playing at shepherdesses in the grounds of a perfectly good boring palace.

Sometimes, against all the odds of their slovenly personal habits, Fulham people marry again. Sometimes people move into Fulham because they have married again, on the principle that they will do it all up and move out again. Fulham husbands open up Fulham lofts to make studios, and Fulham broom cupboards to make third bedrooms. They become bargain hunters and do-it-yourself experts. They change nappies and wash up the tinted glassware and the purple pottery. On Saturdays they are the ones who do the shopping. They buy pet mince for the mutt and carry their babes in arms dressed in blue anoraks around boutiques selling cut-price herbs, dried flowers and reject china. They remove their real flowers to make carports and their window frames to make picture windows so they can better see what improvements are being made to the identical house' opposite.

This is all very reassuring. DIY creates a bond between Fulham men, who are full of outward self-satisfaction and inward nagging doubts. Fulham men become entirely dependent for gratification on their men friends, leaving Fulham women free to find their gratification amongst their women friends. In Earl's Court this would be perverted, in Putney it would be suburban, in Fulham it is plain macho. Fulham men plan outings to the local pub for a game of darts and go to the snooker club without their wives. They support Fulham Football Club precisely because it is not Chelsea. They enjoy seeing Fulham lose. If Fulham wins and Chelsea starts losing they switch allegiances and go to Stamford Bridge. This subtly distinguishes the Fulham arriviste from the indigenous working class, who never want to see their team lose. In the end this distinction separates the men from the boys. Fulham husbands who enjoy the amateur role stay put. Fulham husbands who don't move out to Putney or up to town. Fulham wives always stay put.

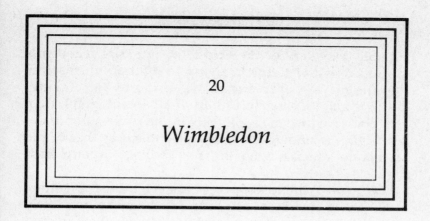

20

Wimbledon

WIMBLEDON HAS THE good fortune to be neither right in
town nor right in the country, which should mean that it
enjoys the best of both worlds. Its orderly houses are set
well apart, and its wide open spaces are easily accessible.
Wimbledon people are well aware of this privilege and
aim to guard it rigidly. This means that they grow up to be
very stuffy and narrow-minded. They are afraid of the
bright lights and agoraphobic about wide open spaces,
and their whole aim in adulthood is to curtail the potential
of both.

The annual embodiment of this aim takes place at the
All England Lawn Tennis and Croquet Club. This is a
wide open space in Wimbledon, crammed for two weeks
in June with as many people as possible, who, despite the
physical discomfort and mental excitement attached to the
tennis championships they have turned out to see, are
expected to behave rather as if they were at a Sunday
afternoon tea party with an octogenarian maiden aunt.
Needless to say, such temperamental stars of the turf as
John McEnroe and Ilie Nastase are not the only ones who
fail to shape up. Tempers run high amongst the audience
too, as do spirits. Countless members faint, flail, ooh, aah,
shout and scream beneath the haughty gaze of umpires

specially elevated for the occasion. And local schoolgirls spend the entire fortnight trying to infiltrate themselves into the players' changing rooms (male) to beg an autograph if not a jockstrap, or best of all an autograph on a jockstrap. Neither the well-being of the players nor of the schoolgirls is undermined nearly as much as that of the stuffy old officials who are not in line for any such requests.

Stuffy old Wimbledon people are committed to getting their young in line at an early age to make absolutely certain they grow up to be just as stuffy as they are and never have such a good time again. This is done by means of a Proper Education. Wimbledon is full of private schools and colleges where shapely young ladies on the brink of teenage adventures are crammed into shapeless gymslips, required to sing hymns about eternal virtue, to walk in crocodiles (not run) wear their hair in unremarkable styles and generally aspire to all the nineteenth-century decencies which it is universally assumed enable you to parse Latin sentences and decline French verbs. This is not an easy thing for young ladies. Once they get the whiff of oxygen in their lungs from all the Wimbledon open spaces, they are less inclined to behave like demure *demoiselles* than unbridled colts. They do this on the tennis court, on the netball court, on the rounders and hockey fields and on horseback, and above all on the common on nature walks. Nature walks in Wimbledon mean one thing to young Wimbledon ladies undergoing a decent education, and quite another to those prematurely senile teachers charged with providing it. While generations of proper spinsters are busy lecturing their pupils on the brilliant natural packaging of frog spawn or the aerodynamic properties of the sycamore seed, their classes are apt to be concentrating on a much more interesting phenomenon of Mother Nature which traditionally takes place in Wimbledon. Unless you are entirely familiar with the area this may not be what you immediately think.

The major Wimbledon phenomenon is known among aficionados as Wombling, after the nursery characters, and as such it presents a totally innocent aspect to those who wish to see innocence in it. Wombling, any educated child might assume, can only take place on Wimbledon Common between a lot of fictional furry animals with names like Bonaparte and Tobermory. Thus the greatest objection of retarded spinster teachers is that such a sport is far too infantile for young ladies whose parents are paying a good deal of money well earned on the Stock Exchange to groom them to sit for Classics Scholarships to Oxford and Cambridge. 'Grow up, Angela,' the natural history mistress is apt to say when she overhears secretive whisperings on the subject; or, 'Isn't it time you had your mind on higher things?' Angela meanwhile is completely overcome by the giggles while Samantha can scarcely concentrate on breathing to keep alive.

Despite these assumptions, Wombling actually takes place on Wimbledon Common between consenting males who are completely unknown to each other, sometimes after dark, but preferably in broad daylight and is especially thrilling if it is observed by the entire Upper IV. On fine summer days during the lunch hour entire trains leave Earl's Court on the District Line packed with potential Womblers wearing figure-hugging T-shirts, dangerously restrictive underwear, neat moustaches and short proper haircuts and carrying folded copies of the *Daily Telegraph* in their picnic baskets. Womblers, though all bent on variations of the same thing, must never speak to each other on the train. Instead they wait till they arrive in Wimbledon Station, whence they all set off towards the common separately, past the proper colleges for young ladies, past the well-named Wimbledon Conservative

Association and the Papal Pro-Nunciate. The idea that
Wombling is about to take place on such obviously
sacrosanct territory rather than in the sleazy back alleys of
Earl's Court is especially important to the proper enjoyment of the occasion. Womblers scatter into the bracken,
the silver birch and the brambles and set to the thrilling
task of flushing out other Womblers who have taken their
fancy aboard the train.

The rules of Wombling are very rigid, as is appropriate
to every Wimbledon sport. Womblers must never resort to
such banal methods of intercourse as mere conversation.
They must never exchange names, never mind addresses.
They must vow never to repeat their performances with
the same Womblers again. Whatever they get up to is
defined only in sign language, whereby an appropriately
hung bunch of keys or a coloured handkerchief denotes
some preference which is a mystery to all but the
Womblers themselves—and the well-bred Wimbledon
ladies, of course. The nature notebooks of these young
ladies are much fuller of such social observations than of
the mating habits of the female cuckoo or the reproductive
cycle of the rabbit. Wimbledon school mistresses who go
on nature walks because of their powers of observation
somehow fail to notice this sort of thing. Even if it is
brought directly to their attention they manage to turn a
blind eye to it, probably because most of them are living in
blithely unconventional circumstances anyway with the
gym mistress.

Angela and Samantha meanwhile emerge from the
whole thing completely unscathed, notwithstanding the
usual extra-curricular research they conduct with their
best friends at weekends. This involves the customary
harassment of conventional courting couples by creeping
up through the long grass and catching them at it. They
then pedal furiously away on their bicycles in time for tea.

Having ascertained at an early age that all adults are completely disgusting Angela and Samantha are then all set to marry into proper Wimbledon society and to procreate in the acceptable local manner. Wimbledon babies are found under gooseberry bushes by fully clothed adults in Ascot hats and pin-striped trousers. They are immediately kitted out in grey serge or purple sackcloth and sent to proper Wimbledon colleges so the whole cycle can begin again.

21

Ruislip

THE SUBURBS, IT has been said, are one of the most brilliant inventions of the twentieth century. The finger of urban squalor never pointed as far as Ruislip, Pinner, Surbiton or East Sheen. Not for them the delinquent shadow of the 'Sixties high rises, nor the left-over maze of the Victorian slum. Not for them the feudal inequalities of the open countryside. In the suburbs each man has his similar patch, each wife her child, each child its dog, each bird its bath, each garden its rockery, each rockery its gnome. The suburbs are a microcosm of perfection.

Fifty years after their planning, the almond avenues have blossomed, the grass has matured, and generations of bluetits have learned to turn upside down on generations of half coconuts; and the suburbs assault you with this perfection. The pollen tickles the nostrils, the ozone spurs the step while the spray-on Simoniz reflects the perfectly endless rows of perfectly identical Tudorbethan three-ups and two-downs in perfect states of repair. Scarcely a façade without its Snowcem, a lawn without its stripes, a border without its slug pellets, a patio without its deckchair. Scarcely a garden *with* a vegetable patch. The suburbs are against real life. All-caring, vigilante suburban man is on the warpath against loud music, foul footpaths, rusty bodywork, copious greenfly and garish gables—especially other people's. Only the slight disarray of the whiter than white nylon net curtains points to the imperfections of some human beings. The suburbs are as proper as the ambitions of average man. On the surface, that is. Transplant a feminist to Ruislip and she will seem like the perfect wife and mother. Transplant a spy and he will be the mainspring of the commuter club. A ripper will take orders, a pederast run the PTA, a lesbian the WI, a swinger will appoint himself marriage counsellor, an alcoholic will serve behind the counter at the pub. People may wonder about them, speculate about them, hallucinate about them; they may stick their eyes to keyholes in pursuit of vicarious thrills, walk their dogs or post their letters at improbable hours, but suburban people will never ask questions of the people concerned. This is because they do not want to hear the answers. Metroland is the promised land and never must the fear be actually voiced that the milk and honey could actually dry up. Metroland was named for the Metropolitan Line, which was wrongly named since it appears to have something to do with town. Metroman would be carried away from the sins of the city upon it, together with his two and a fraction children, to a land of dreams as surely as if it were Disneyland, a place where the goldfish never turn into piranhas, the tea-roses to Venus fly-traps, nor the *Daily Mail* to the *Morning Star*, because the inhabitants never quite grow up.

In exchange for this perfection Metroman sacrificed his proper roots. Since he no longer knows where he comes from he is doubly uncertain about everyone else. This makes Metroman suspicious of everyone but uncertain quite what to do about it. Metroman is not action man except when it comes to moving someone else's car from his grass verge. In Ruislip, Pinner, Surbiton and East

Sheen people never actually move their own cars if they can help it. Ruislip people know that the only good Honda is the Honda in a garage. In the garage the car may be preserved as long as possible as a symbol of their earning power rather than their mobility, which they have sacrificed by moving to the suburbs. You may get under a car and fiddle with it, or on top of the car and fiddle with it, you may drive it to the station once a month at a pinch, you may take it on Sunday as far as the end of the road. But you must never, never park it on the street in front of some alien privet no matter what emergency may prompt you. This leads to car wars. Car wars last for ever once they have been declared. Similarly dog wars and the wars of the roses. Alien dogs are forever damned, or dogged, and woe betide the child that beheads your semi-standard, Peace. Since Ruislip people never ask questions they never get the explanations for any piece of behaviour even if it is accidental. Ruislip people make statements. 'That child will come to a sticky end,' they pronounce. 'He is pale, she is too thin, she is a lovely girl, he has let the side down. She is going to be a doctor. He should go on the stage. As good as anything I have seen on television any time.'

Most of these statements involve children. This is because children are the right size for Ruislip. Suburban people who live in Lilliputian houses have to cut everything down to size. Conifers are dwarves, poodles are miniatures, glasses are thimbles, books are digested and records highlighted. Small things are controllable and suburban people like to be in control at all times. Metroman only drinks in public at Christmas—and then only one glass—he never speaks of drugs, foreigners, foreign food, the Pope or party politics. He speaks about the weather and the Queen. Too much speaking is out in Metroland, but then so is too much silence. Should a benign silence once descend in Ruislip, someone is bound to say, quite unexpectedly, 'Isn't it nice and quiet?' This will be repeated by the budgie, granny and by mother, who will add, 'Shall we all have a nice cup of tea?' She will then turn on the television.

Television has naturally taken over the focal point of any room and will be placed in front of the artificial gas fire or in the centre of the bay window. Ruislip people do not make any attempt to follow any of the programmes, however. Anyone who looks too deeply into an apparent plot is immediately offered a fairy cake. Ruislip people never have any time to be hungry. They are always being offered a good square meal. No sooner have they finished breakfast than someone is peeling the sprouts for lunch. No sooner has everyone's plate been cleared than the tea trolley appears. No sooner has the trolley been emptied than on comes high tea. Ruislip people love eating because they love washing up. Town people hate washing up. In Chelsea, Islington and Hampstead no one ever washes up if they can help it. They like to be invited out. If they are not invited out they simply go out. Chelsea, Islington and Hampstead people would rather eat out all the time than ever do any washing up. They would rather go out to breakfast (or not come home in time for it) than ever wash up a coffee cup. In Ruislip, Pinner, Surbiton and East Sheen they start washing up before they have finished eating. When they have finished washing the dishes they take down the curtains. In between courses they do the Hoovering. Ruislip people bring out the Hoover in between every home-made sponge. They bring it out if you put on a record òr dare to open a book. When they have finished Hoovering around your ankles they queue up to show you their do-it-yourself carpet laying, their do-it-yourself developing and the kitten picture they bought for fivepence at the church bazaar. They show you the garden with the do-it-yourself workshop at the bottom. Or they show you the toilet. There is absolutely no need to show anyone in Ruislip the toilet since they can certainly find it themselves. Ruislip toilets are always marked by a ceramic tile in pink, blue or yellow which may or may not have a bullfighter on it saying something like, 'Penny for your thoughts', 'Smallest room', or 'Ancestral seat'.

Inside the toilet it will be very cosy. There will be a candlewick cosy on the seat and a matching candlewick cosy on the floor. The Airwick will be suction cupped behind the rosebud curtains and the water in the cistern will run baby blue. Do not be tempted to linger in this haven. In Clapham, Muswell Hill and Barnes you get a pine bookshelf next to the washbasin containing a few lewd books, magazines with the odd mention of the householder, and last week's Sunday papers. Woe betide you if you come back to the assembled company without having fathomed the point of the display. In Ruislip, Pinner, Surbiton and East Sheen, nothing of the sort. Any unexplained absence will be put down to undue curiosity about the upstairs décor. Ruislip people get very fidgety if you take an unreasonable amount of time over your ablutions. At which point they are liable to sprint stealthily upstairs and catch you appraising the candlewick bedspreads and the orange geometric bedroom wallpaper. Ruislip people know that this is what you will be doing because this is what they would be doing themselves rather than ask to see the bedroom wallpaper.

Ruislip people enjoy their silent sleuthing and they enjoy following other people in their attempts to do their own silent sleuthing. They put up huge fences around their property, or giant hollyhocks to encourage curiosity. Ruislip people always keep their telephones by the front door in the hall. This is so that every telephone conversation can be monitored without it actually going on record that it is being monitored. A telephone conversation in the living room must either be overtly avoided or deliberately overheard. A telephone conversation in the bedroom is always bound to be discreet. But a telephone conversation in the hall offers the sort of challenge to subterfuge that Ruislip minds adore. The moment a Ruislip telephone rings, doors open all over the place in Ruislip semis. People who were previously perfectly happy reading the serial in *Woman's Own*, will immediately cross the hallway, ostensibly to make a cup of tea. People washing the upstairs windows—and meanwhile taking a peek at the state of the nextdoor garden—will suddenly remember they have to bring in the milk or put out the cat. This entails passing the telephone on tiptoe. When they have heard what they have overheard Ruislip people will never mention it to the person who has said it, but they will wonder, speculate, hallucinate and quietly conclude the absolute worst. It is always the way in the suburbs. Concluding the worst is the natural reaction to living with permanent perfection. I wonder if the town planners ever realised that living with perfection would be such a strain?

22

Blackheath

BLACKHEATH HAS BEEN united with Hampstead in its
own mind ever since Jack Straw (whose memory is
perpetuated by a pub on Hampstead Heath), joined with
Wat Tyler to assemble the Peasants' Revolt on Blackheath
in 1381, more than six hundred years ago. Tyler was
stabbed and Straw beheaded, which is why 'black' is a
good adjective for the place. Blackheath still feels pretty
sore about peasants. These days the funny little fellows
leave their lower-class litter all over the well-named
common land and park their vulgar vehicles on its verges.
Some of them even dare to stop and have a cup of tea on
the Heath on their way to the Costa del Sol via Dover after
struggling through the traffic on the Old Kent Road. As an
alternative to homicide, Blackheath is trying to discourage
this sort of behaviour by cleaning up the caff where they
pursue these horrible habits. Such élitist gestures make
those proletarian peasants even more determined to picnic
where they will. On every anniversary of the Revolt they
determine to congregate on the common. They still seem
to think it belongs to them despite parliamentary interven-
tion in the early 1800s to parcel most of it off to the
aristocrats to encourage the disinherited commoner to
work in their factories. With every anniversary of the

Revolt, Blackheath people become more and more determined to put an end to the practice of peasant congrega-
tion.

Blackheath is an oasis of culture, surrounded on three
sides by places Blackheath people can hardly bring themselves to mention, which is why they feel so defensive. In
fact they are called Lewisham (which is famous for its
National Health Hospital), Kidbrook (which is famous for
its comprehensive school) and Charlton (which is famous
for its football club), none of which is any real reason to be
famous as far as Blackheath people are concerned. On the
fourth side Blackheath looks down on Greenwich, which
is as it should be because Greenwich is famous for being
Royal. Blackheath people may be culture snobs but they
are also liberals. Liberals are people who are very broad-
minded but who object to absolutely everything. (This
makes it possible to be both élitist and public spirited.)

Liberals do not like anything which sounds like fun,
especially if it presupposes an element of personal choice.
Liberals do not like people who smoke or drive because
they pollute the public air. They do not like people who
are happily married because they assume they must be
boring. They do not like children who are well-behaved
because they assume they must be retarded. They do not
like children who are badly behaved because they attract
too much attention. They do not like children. They do not
like inherited wealth because they haven't inherited any,
nor conspicuous consumption because it is vulgar. They
are in favour of supplementary benefit in theory: in
practice they could not live on it. They do not like council
architecture because it has no aesthetic merit. Nor do they
like council tenants, especially if they come to Blackheath
and drop cigarette ends and ill-mannered children all over
their Heath.

So far, so Hampstead. But Blackheath, outside the

cultural catchment area of the London underground, is also commuter country. Commuters are dedicated to convenience. One outstanding Blackheath convenience is the architectural mutation known as the Span house. Span houses, and their many imitations, Span-ish houses, are terrifying quadrangles composed of identical boxes designed to hold Span man, who will be an early achiever; his community-minded Span wife who dresses at Laura Ashley; and two Span children called Sophie and Jason. Span children go to the Montessori school followed by Blackheath High or a boarding school if they pass the exam, and Kidbrook Comprehensive if they do not. At this point their parents will become ardent supporters of socialist education theories and the wife will lose interest in housework.

Span people may keep a Span dog (pedigree), a Span cat (tabby), unless Sophie has been found to be allergic to them, which is a good attention-getter. Span achievers will be Oxbridge people who are so used to popping in and out of each others' college sets, borrowing each others' clothes, essays, wives and girlfriends, that living cheek by jowl in a lot of nesting boxes in Blackheath makes no difference to them at all. Span achievers will be theatre people attracted by the Greenwich theatre, conservationists attracted by the Heath, media people attracted by the idea that Blackheath is like Hampstead, advertising people attracted by Span advertising, and architects attracted by the idea that living in the reflected glory of Vanbrugh and Wren gives some sort of validity to their admiration for more contemporary cultural heroes like Buckminster Fuller, Frank Lloyd Wright, Mies Van der Rohe and Walter Gropius.

For some of Blackheath architecture is very lovely indeed—the pre-Span stuff. Blackheath is a remarkable pocket of Georgian, Victorian and Edwardian elegance.

There are vast stretches of Blackheath where it is almost impossible for the eye to fall on a less than felicitous sight—architecturally speaking, that is. It is a strange rule of thumb that people who live in beautiful houses are not beautiful people. Blackheath is full of beautiful houses. Blackheath looks like one of those Ackermann prints that middle-class professionals invariably hang on their walls the moment they leave university to remind them and others of better days spent frolicking in the heady carelessness of May Balls and punting to the rare accompaniment of madrigals on a medieval lute.

Blackheath is not full of beautiful people, but of middle-class professionals. In their student days did such people dress to complement the lines of the Wren library or the classicism of the Ashmolean façade? No, they most certainly did not. Did they wear wing collars and tailored outfits? Did they wear gowns and college scarves? They wore neither if they could help it. Elegance was considered decadent, uniforms insensitive. Those people who wore wing collars became art dealers and went happily to live in Belgravia. Those people who wore college scarves became history masters and went to live unhappily in Twickenham.

Blackheath is both well-to-do and bohemian. Well-to-do people kit themselves out in Yves St Laurent and live in modern copies of architectural gems. Bohemians live in damp lofts and practise mind over matter. Well-to-do bohemians find genuine architectural gems and live in them as if they were damp lofts. Well-to-do people have a highly developed sense of personal aesthetics. Bohemians have a highly developed sense of personal aesthetics (even though you may not share it), but well-to-do bohemians have no sense of personal aesthetics whatsoever. Well-to-do people dye their hair, co-ordinate their clothes and match their paintings to their curtains. Bohemians dye their hair, mix their clothes and hang their paintings where their curtains should be. Well-to-do bohemians are simply not aware of their hair, their clothes, their paintings and their curtains. Such things are peripheral visual vanities which have nothing to do with the real cerebral stuff of life, which is, as with Hampstead people, the endless distillation of the correct attitude. The correct attitude to such things as Dr Jolly, French holidays, the Jacobean theatre, pedestrian thoroughfares, ecology, the Southern Railway and Martin Amis. All this goes to show that Blackheath people may be literate and articulate but they quite simply have no grasp at all of some of the most basic facts of pleasurable life. The basic facts are that people who live against weathered brick façades, glorious green expanses and stuccoed white pillars, as they do, should wear toning tawny clothes and cultivate an attractive stance. Blackheath people wear purple clothes and slouch around in second-hand furs from Oxfam furtively collecting for Oxfam. (This is called 'recycling'.) It is impossible to visit Blackheath without marvelling at the proliferation of purple which they manage to find even when it has been out of vogue since the 1920s. Blackheath people are privy to purple anoraks, purple sweaters, purple tights, socks and headscarves.

If red is the colour of passion and green the colour of jealousy, purple must be the colour of the intellect. Blackheath people are neither passionate nor jealous, because they are far too intelligent, but this does not mean they do not have affairs. If anything it means they have more affairs. Affairs of the body, excluding the heart, are a favourite pastime in Blackheath. The very fact of them is essential and the essence is that the facts should be made as public as possible. This means that there is an enormous amount of public sex in Blackheath. It is firstly in an attempt to arouse the dormant passion of jealousy, and secondly because of the proximity of the place to nature. No matter where you are in Blackheath, or how close to each other, it is impossible not to glimpse a blade of grass, a tree or even a pond. All this makes Blackheath people very frisky. There is endless intertwining of Huskies in the High Street, hand-holding over nut cutlets and intimate exchanges while apparently gazing in the bookshop windows at the Ackermann prints, the bad watercolours and the Victorian volumes about local history.

Preferably this is done with someone else's marriage partner. Blackheath may apparently provide the perfect family environment, its roads may be humped with sleeping policemen to protect Blackheath dogs at play, but Blackheath parents do as much as possible to put the nucleus of the family at risk. This is because, theoretically at least, Blackheath people know their partners are far too intelligent to mind them indulging in a little tomfoolery with someone from outside the marriage, as long as he or she lives in Blackheath. If their partners really do appear not to mind, Blackheath people try to force them to mind by the process of graphic confession which should ideally take place in front of two children, one mother-in-law, the goldfish and the dog. Not only does the whole family soon learn about Blackheath affairs, but the whole of Blackheath and no doubt the whole of the rest of London too. This is because Blackheath people have powerful media connections, and there is nothing at all media people can keep quiet about, which is why they are media people in the first place. Media people gossip about other media people and other media people gossip about media people and they all pretend they are outraged by the invasion of their privacy.

They are much more outraged if no one bothers to invade it. This would mean that they were not worth gossiping about. Blackheath people would far rather be unhappy and the subject of a little idle gossip than cold-shouldered by the wagging tongue. A smidgen of poignant unhappiness sets Blackheath people apart from other suburban people, who are obsessed with nothing more traumatic than rose-pruning and rearranging their garden gnomes. People in Span houses do not buy gnomes. They are very casual about their gardens. They are very casual about their décor. They fill their houses with musty old books. They review modern books for a living and sell them on to booksellers who sell them on to people who live in Barnes and use them as wallpaper. People in Blackheath sell their review copies to draw attention to themselves as reviewers, and not because they are ever very poor.

For, quite apart from their investment in Blackheath, they are more than likely to own some lovely little place in south-west France or just outside Lucca. It is a fact of Blackheath life that very few people ever get to see this little place apart from its immediate owners. Blackheath people say this is because it is so make-shift they would be too ashamed. They explain that they spend their summers, like Hampstead people, sleeping with spiders and drawing water from a far-distant well. This is called 'pleading genteel poverty' in order to arouse admiration rather than resentment. In actual fact the little place is more than likely to boast a couple of hundred hectares not to mention a swimming pool and its own wine-press. Blackheath people tend to disappear all summer only to come back in the autumn with a deep tan and their own personalised château-bottled wine-lists. They rather apologetically flog the wine to their friends to make a little money on the side. They explain how they are saving up to buy their own cesspool and describe how they have dug the earth with their own bare hands and trodden the grapes with their own dirty feet. No mention is ever made of the family of old retainers including the poolman, master vintner, landscape gardener and locally renowned cook whose daughter is also the upstairs maid. Blackheath people are wise investors and make the most of the money from their early achievements.

Sometimes this secret affinity to property is the subject of an unfortunate revelation which Blackheath man might initially enjoy. This is when he meets someone else's Hampstead wife by accident in some French market town where her family also has a (genuinely) small and primitive place in the country. If both of them are currently enjoying a little rest and recuperation without their partners, or even if they are enjoying it *with* their partners, such a meeting will almost certainly lead to more frequent subsequent ones. The frequent subsequent meetings will not be limited to a reciprocal stimulation of grey matter. To Blackheath man the most elevated form of sexual affair to which he can aspire is with a Hampstead wife, given his atavistic orientation to her environment. This is not an affair which he lightly puts aside, and his own wife may be forced to play her trump card which you can be sure will have something to do with the property. She will probably throw him out. Blackheath wives are umbilically joined to their property since they know they are unlikely to find anything quite as nice twice in a lifetime.

In Blackheath they say that whenever you see a 'For Sale' sign on a house it is a sure sign of a divorce in the family. It is not the only sign, because Blackheath wives move heaven and earth to stay where they are. They dig in, stay put and carry on their own less destructive petty local affairs. Meanwhile Span man, or Vanbrugh man, far from moving up in the world to Hampstead, is forced to put his château on the market and shack up, suitably chastened, in a cramped Edwardian terrace in the clone country of Clapham.

23

Barbican

I HAVE ALWAYS found the City of London a most romantic place, even though, or probably because, I did my very first job there, which was sticking down envelopes in a very minor anteroom of the Head Office of the National Westminster Bank. Since I was rarely occupied at board-room level in the lunch hour or whisked to some choice place like Le Poulbot to exchange financial views with some City whiz, there was plenty of time to potter around the perimeter of the very first London settlement, with what remained of its landmarks, newer institutions and even newer bomb-sites. I became particularly fond of the bomb-sites—as an inevitability after the event—largely because they were oases of buddleia and birdsong amid the formalities of town, which extended a welcome invitation to prolong the hours of misspent youth. My fondness led to a search for somewhere to live in the area, so it was with personal interest that I looked forward to the burgeoning of the Barbican out of the buddleia.

Burgeon it did, and burgeoning it still is. Barbican residents have hardly been without the sound of burgeoning since they moved in, with bulldozers on bass, pneumatic drills on vibes and vocals by construction workers on extended tea-breaks, and modern workmanship being what it is this will no doubt go on long after it is ostensibly finished, which to all intents and purposes it now is.

The result is mysterious.

The Barbican, even on a good day, is rather like one of those unfathomable excavated Roman towns which presumably were once full of working fountains, sophisticated conduits and idle citizens lingering among the colonnades while ducks and dogs chased each other all over the open spaces. Apart from the idleness very little is fulfilled. There are very few dogs in the Barbican: they are not allowed. There are too few ducks. The ducks were discouraged by the fact that the ornamental lake—or rather the rectilinear stagnant pool—was empty for a couple of years before they filled it for the official opening of the Arts Centre. One day the residents of the Barbican looked out of their perfectly planned windows over their perfectly planned balconies to see that the perfectly planned water had somehow drained away. With the water went the fish and with the fish went the ducks. The construction workers returned (noisily) to shore up the foundations at a whispered cost of nearly a quarter of a million pounds.

Much whispering goes on in the Barbican: it is a tone of voice encouraged by ancient monuments and brand-new showcases. Haphazard in-between living arrangements have their own vitality, but the very old and the very new exude the quality of a sepulchre where living people raise their voices at their peril. In the Barbican complete silence is encouraged except for certain artificial days which are set apart for festivals of outmoded freaks like fire-eaters. This is called 'being community-minded'. In most communities, from Barnes to Hampstead, the whole idea of the community is fostered by regular contact over the garden wall or at the wine and cheese parties. Barbican visitors pay outlandish prices for the dubious privilege of a piece of mouldy Cheddar, a cup of watery coffee and a wary glimpse of some foreign stranger the other end of the water garden. Barbican residents, young and old, are not surprisingly obsessed with preserving their snobbish tranquillity in the face of this invasion, like a bunch of bad-tempered pensioners determined to keep their relatives at arm's length on visiting day. Barbican residents can be seen eyeing the invasion from beneath their Japanese headsets, which is how they listen to music so as not to disturb the supposed perfect peace of the place.

Disturbing the peace is all too easily done in the Barbican. To start with the walls are paper-thin and the ceilings are so low that a mere baby crawling on the floor above sounds like an army of centurions on the move. Underneath rumbles the tube and in between there is the persistent slamming of heavy security doors. Barbican residents are very security minded. They speak in capital letters of Much Machinery designed to set the Residents Apart from the Interlopers: of Keys, Housekeepers, Systems, Night Patrols and Deadlocks which do not necessarily work. They are security minded because, far from being the homogeneous community intended, the Barbican has been thrown up in an unnatural place which can only be populated by slightly crazy individuals and which is visited daily by a commuting or itinerant population on which there is no easy check. Identical multi-level storeys form a series of anonymous mazes in which footsteps echo suspiciously in the most lion-hearted ears. Young ladies visiting the place are apt to be asked pertinent questions by car park attendants like whether they intend to stay all night, to which the only possible answer is no, if they can possibly find the way out. This is not as easy as it should be since the lifts, even in the Arts Centre, bear no relevant information for a quick get-away: thus the ground floor is billed as Level Three and God only knows how to find a car parked in Car Park Four on Level Two—or is it Six? Eight? One? Many other people have been known to abandon their vehicles and take the nearest passing taxi—if they can find one, and if its lights are not off because it is going home to Hackney.

Apart from this, groups of unidentifiable students are always roaming loutishly around the podium, encouraged by hapless tour guides to marvel at this 'Sixties phenomenon of pre-stained concrete. Hordes of stockbrokers, whose loyalty is above all to Surbiton, hover at lunchtime in the otherwise deserted pubs, and pin-striped paedophiles spend their coffee-breaks waiting to catch a glimpse of a red knee beneath a red gym slip on some girl from the City of London School, which is marooned on a moated island in the midst of the complex like some infant Alcatraz.

When the Barbican first loomed off the drawing board children were an integral part of the scheme. Time was when the town planners conjured up tempting visions of happy acres reverberating to a sound long silenced in the City: the sound of family life. The wailing of children, the scolding of parents, teenage boppings and senile meanderings were to invite a response from the artistic and business communities so the three could blossom in glorious mutual fulfilment and enjoyment of the City's facilities and aims. So the high rises went up, looking in at each other over unseasoned gardens or out over other high rises full of defeated office cactuses crammed among the stencilling machines. Nature has a shallow foothold in the Barbican. There is an absence of buddleia and birdsong. In the interests of hygiene, says the tenants' handbook, residents are asked to refrain from feeding and encouraging the birds. This sort of thing means that there is an absence of art too, for art flourishes not in a Barbican complex, but in an abrasion with life. As a pathetic illustration of this, one perfectly good nineteenth century proscenium theatre a hundred yards from the Barbican is reserved for amateur performances while the new theatre within its complex attempts to drum up business without any of the advantages of history or personality.

The fact is that architects of show places are concerned with themselves rather than the show places. They are concerned with the shell of their invention and not the reality of it. Show places must be seen to work, even if they demonstrably do not, in order to encourage the business of the architects. This means that many artistes, who should know better, are lured to impossible venues, where they demonstrate to people who are not willing to listen because of the price of the building and of the seats, that their skill does not necessarily work in unsympathetic circumstances. No matter. Architects endeavour to train people to understand their buildings rather than the buildings being an evolution of human error. Thus normal human behaviour is discouraged in practice within designer precincts while it is theoretically encouraged. Children are among the first to spot this discrepancy. And grown-ups are the first to spot when it is inconvenient to have children. Today the children of Barbican residents are fewer and fewer. There is no easy place for them to play. If they do not fall off the balconies there is every possibility they may get trapped in the lifts. If they make it to the ground floor in one piece, they are sure to roller-skate around the hallowed complex. If they stay indoors they will quite simply swamp the tiny flats. Therefore they must be taken to a cage where they can play according to the regulations of the estate. How shall they be taken? Along interminable concrete walkways where there are no pram slopes. Children and mothers move out.

Despite the immense lineage devoted to their virtues,

new arts centres rarely make any difference to the vitality
of a place. What they do is attract still more intense
theoreticians who are obsessed, like the architects, with
the form rather than the content of the art. Three cinemas,
a restaurant complex (not Cordon Bleu), a conservatory
(not Kew) and a theatre are less likely to bring an influx of
real people to the Barbican than the construction of a
Brent-type shopping centre. For one thing, will they all
work? The National Theatre, which has much in common
visually with the Barbican (including the pioneer presence
of Peter Hall who lived in one of its flats), has the
persistent ability to mechanically crack up in the most
foolish fashion. It has been known for the curtain to jam in
mid-performance and for the entire show to be stopped
until an engineer can be sent for all the way from the mid-
west of America. In the Barbican, if the underfloor heating
gets out of control, there is nothing for it but to suffer or
leave home. There is no such thing as an individual on-off
switch in each flat. The waste-disposal unit requires the
turn of mind of an atom scientist—several residents are
reduced to putting the rubbish outside their doors in the
old-fashioned way, from where it is never collected. The
advent of the Number Four bus for those who wish to
leave the area is rather less likely than the English
summer.

Such trivialities do not necessarily deter the ardent
Barbican boor, who is someone who would rather be a
statistic in a rented bedsitter than land himself with a
mortgage and a lot of land. For all that he is as possessive
and defensive of his folly. He takes a masochistic pleasure
in perpetrating a suburban life-style in the centre of town.
He gardens in his window box, frowns on the overt, arty
presence of the Guildhall students of music and drama,
and champions a croquet club on the communal lawn and
a playschool on the eighteenth floor (which, as every

mother knows, is the perfect place for a playschool). He takes a keen interest in the antics in his neighbour's bedroom, which, modern architecture being what it is, invariably overlooks his own sitting room. And he creates smaller and smaller residents' associations to promote the minority interests of one end of one floor of one wing of his own block.

The symbol of the Barbican is a fortress. The word Barbican means a fortress on a city wall. But though the residents may like to think of the Barbican as their own particular fortress on the City of London Wall, the opening of the new cultural centre has changed all that. It has thrown it open to absolutely everyone who can find it, ensuring that those few remaining residents who can bear this state of affairs are exposed more and more, like the occupants of an urban zoo, to the stares of professional tourists. This year the flats are being sold off to potential enthusiasts of this way of life. But Barbican realists acknowledge that this may mean more and more company acquisitions, even though they are theoretically not allowed. What London Wall needs, if it is to survive as a place of pilgrimage, is more commuter trains (and maps) so that office workers can thankfully get there away from the cultural desert of suburbia, and equally thankfully return, leaving the Barbican complex to those true addicts of anonymity who thrive in concrete landscapes. Whether this is a recipe for culture remains to be seen. At present the most profound emotional experience suffered by the coach-loads of curious who always overrun anything new, is their horrified reaction to the livid colour scheme on the restaurant walls.

24

Islington

ISLINGTON IS A failure. As someone once said of the
future, 'I have seen it and it doesn't work.'

Time was when the very name of the place was like a
clarion call on the lips of every middle-class do-gooder in
sight. Like an army of social workers they flocked there in
their hundreds, if not their thousands, spreading the
word through every form of media to hand, since the
media, as it happened, was the area in which this
privileged new race worked. Like all media people,
essentially they were working for each other, though they
themselves put a more generous construction on it. TV
men, ad men, newspaper men, film men, publishers,
playwrights, teachers, politicians—communicators all—
gravitated to snoop and comment, declaim and deplore
and generally busybody around: people for whom it was a
convenience to live in Islington because they worked in
Fleet Street, and people for whom it was a downright
inconvenience because they worked for the BBC in Lime
Grove. We've moved to Islington, they boasted, and the
world—or at least that part of it situated between the
Angel and Highbury—will be a demonstrably better
place. In those days they would never have done the
obvious thing and moved to Shepherd's Bush. Shepherd's

Bush was working-class, but not that working-class. It was cosy compared to Islington, part of the Candlewick Belt where ducks could proudly fly up *eau-de-nil* chimney breasts and the flock-covered memorial Spanish bull sit reminiscently on the sideboard. They were militant, these middle-class saviours who were to set their sights on Islington, and they would be wasted on their parents' suburbs from which they had just escaped. Not for them the immaculate verges of Metroland, nor the tasteful conversion of some relatively recent terrace near the river.

Islington, by contrast with these things, was interesting because it was downright squalid. It was gloomy, Victorian and urban. Islington people were enthralled by the pall of industrial filth, by the challenge of rude lower-class manners and racial squabbles. Here was an opportunity, verily, for a brave new world. It was also cheap. Dirt cheap. So this over-educated, grant-educated bourgeoisie moved in, theoreticians to a man (and even more so, theoreticians to a woman), with letters after their name from any institution which would have them, full of untried ideals, the aggrandisement that comes from much reading and little doing, and the conviction that now they had all come along nothing would ever be quite the same again. No matter what the conclusions of history, the twentieth century (or at least their part of it) would be an altogether different thing. They were the first generation of physically untroubled, entirely pampered people, yearning to get their lily-white hands dirty in someone else's kitchen sink.

They would teach the drunks not to drink, the smokers not to smoke, the vandals not to vandalise. They would teach mothers not to be housebound, children not to be dependent, men not to be competitive and couples not to be parents. They would teach the sick to get well and the illiterate to write prize-winning literature. They would persuade everyone of every age, creed, sex, colour and class to live in some all-caring, thrusting, flowering, throbbing, aching human community, where pubs were for theatre, not for beer, where markets were for books, not groceries, where streets were for playing in and not for cars. And all this would be dirt cheap if not completely free, since for these offspring of the welfare state it always had been; it would be gloriously, vibrantly, emotionally aesthetic. They would strip all the intervening layers of hypocrisy from all the Victorian pine in their lives and generally evoke the grandeur once more of that era, for Victoriana with all its double standards was curiously what they craved.

They moved into their Victorian slums with their children with their Victorian names, with their Lucys and their Emmas and their Posys and their Rosys. They hung their Victorian pictures on their Victorian walls and reclined on their re-covered Victorian chaise-longues. The Victorian age was a curious model to take because it was the age above all of the haves and the have-nots, of the workhouse poor and the patrician rich. In their own spoiled actuality they sought reality in nostalgia. They were crusading like the Victorians, and patronising, and, if not sentimental, self-deluding. They would turn water into cheap white wine and, for their next trick, into Perrier water. The Victorian age is what they got. Nothing much has changed in Islington, except the rates which go up and up to pay for its pretensions. The working classes are still the working classes and the middle classes are still the middle classes. The working classes hang net curtains over their windows to retain their privacy and blanket them with thick velours through which can still be seen the flicker of the rented colour television with accompanying video and 26-inch screen. The middle classes throw open their shutters to show how accessible they are, hang Tiffany paper lamps from their damp-soiled ceilings, entertain their friends to wine and cheese and don't have anything as vulgar as a television set.

If anything the squalor has rubbed off on the middle classes rather than the other way round. Islington children have Islington accents, and learn nothing much at school; Islington mothers are not very houseproud, Islington men are not all that tough. Islington people do not notice these things about themselves, largely because they are permanently worrying about other people. They worry about old people, young people, very young people, gay people, black people, blue films and circus animals. Do not imagine that all their education has served to make them broad-minded. On the contrary, it has narrowed their views. What these views are doesn't actually matter, because Islington people know they are right whether or not they are borne out by experience. They are right about free schooling and free expression, town planning, playgroups, crèches, community centres, pensioner projects, squats, social security, subsidised fares, legalised abortion, teenage contraception and every form of minority right from Lesbian mothers on pot to public suicides and homosexual divorce. The list is endless because it is paid for by public funds and the public won't pay unless their particular aberration is included. Sometimes they still won't pay, which is why Islington do-gooders have to spend a great deal of time haranguing the unenlightened from the podium rather than going round dispensing a little personal old-fashioned (cheaper) charity to the obviously needy, which was the solution of their Victorian forefathers.

Never mind the facts, let us look at the theories. Islington people know that public support in the form of subsidies and grants is the answer because The Grant paid for their very existence. It paid for their births, their orange juice, their schooling and their degree in social sciences from some peripheral college of further education from which they got their theories. Despite the fact that this education was expensive it was obviously so poor that Islington people are unable to make the connection between their expensively gained views and the expensive results of them. They don't understand what it is that makes life so unbearable for the Islington rate-payer. At the same time, now they are grown up they are the people who are paying the rates and the taxes and everything else which fund things like the demonstrably ineffectual education of their own children.

No wonder they are so confused. They do not realise that more expensive pedestrian precincts will lead to children playing in them rather than going to the expensively erected adventure playground which is too much of a walk away. They do not realise that when children play in the streets they punt their footballs through any window which gets in the way. They do not realise that when streets are blocked off in the interest of aesthetics they are also blocked off from the fire brigade which cannot gain easy access in the case of emergency. They do not realise any of these things until they happen, and even then they argue it must be the practical appliance of the theory which has gone wrong rather than the theory itself. In the case of the fire brigade this is a pity, since Islington people appear to specialise in arson. Either that or they are very accident-prone. Islington is full of burned-out and gutted buildings. Islington people donate thousand-pound videos to their local schools but they cannot prevent their local thieves from taking them away. They may resist decimalisation in their own pubs—yes, they do—but they cannot prevent the rest of the country from coming to more realistic conclusions.

Islington people are not very realistic. They are very

vocal, but not being very realistic is not something you may expect them to sound off about. Even when personally disillusioned they shelter publicly behind the urge to merge their responsibilities with everyone else's. Even when they desperately yank their ignorant offspring from the local schools, they silently send them to board in the country with never a comment against the system. Even when they no longer speak up about Islington as Jerusalem they do not lose the hope that it may rise again not far away. They cast their eyes at other areas with a more forlorn ring to their names where their sporting idealism may still be thought to be in with a chance: in Holloway, they wistfully speculate, in Hackney, in Finsbury, they might buy the egalitarian dream. They will find out how to fund Utopia at no personal cost. They will have to. They are cheap. They are dirt cheap. Their search for new Utopias continues, but it is a curiously fickle process: they were the first aboard the SDP bandwagon and the first to desert the ship the moment she sprung a leak.

Islington is a failure, but the best thing you can say about it is that Islington people do not give up easily.